BRITAIN IN OLD PHOTOGRAPHS

# BLACK COUNTRY
## CHAPELS
### A THIRD SELECTION

### NED WILLIAMS

THE LOCAL HISTORY COMPANY

The Local History Company
an imprint of The History Press
Cirencester Road · Chalford · Stroud
Gloucestershire · GL6 8PE

First published 2008

**British Library Cataloguing in Publication Data**
A catalogue record for this book is available from the
British Library.

ISBN 978-0-7509-4665-0

Typeset in 10.5/13.5 Photina.
Typesetting and origination by
The History Press.
Printed and bound in England by Ashford Colour Press Ltd.

*Title page photograph:* Chapel life extended in all directions to include many diverse activities and in the case of the Primitive Methodists at Greets Green the Sunday School embraced an annual carnival celebration. This was held every October and was organised by Ivy Green (see page 82), and made good use of Farley Park. This picture was taken on 3 October 1953 when Rita Hill was the Carnival Queen. She is surrounded by Betty Middleton, Shirley Icke, Barbara Smith, Linda Thompson, Jean Simmonds, Irene Nightingale, Barbara Woodward, Rita Jacks and Joan Smith. *(Anne Pitt/Ivy Round Archive)*

# THE BLACK COUNTRY SOCIETY

The Black Country Society is proud to be associated with **Sutton Publishing** of Stroud. In 1994 the society was invited by Sutton Publishing to collaborate in what has proved to be a highly successful publishing partnership, namely the extension of the *Britain in Old Photographs* series into the Black Country. In this joint venture the Black Country Society has played an important role in establishing and developing a major contribution to the region's photographic archives by encouraging society members to compile books of photographs of the area or town in which they live.

The first book in the Black Country series was *Wednesbury in Old Photographs* by Ian Bott, launched by Lord Archer of Sandwell in November 1994. Since then almost 70 Black Country titles have been published. The total number of photographs contained in these books is in excess of 13,000, suggesting that the whole collection is probably the largest regional photographic survey of its type in any part of the country to date.

This voluntary society was founded in 1967 as a reaction to the trends of the late 1950s and early '60s. This was a time when the reorganisation of local government was seen as a threat to the identity of individual communities and when, in the name of progress and modernisation, the industrial heritage of the Black Country was in danger of being swept away.

The general aims of the society are to stimulate interest in the past, present and future of the Black Country, and to secure at regional and national levels an accurate understanding and portrayal of what constitutes the Black Country and, wherever possible, to encourage and facilitate the preservation of the Black Country's heritage.

The society, which now has over 2,500 members worldwide, organises a yearly programme of activities. There are six venues in the Black Country where evening meetings are held on a monthly basis from September to April. In the summer months, there are fortnightly guided evening walks in the Black Country and its green borderland, and there is also a full programme of excursions further afield by car. Details of all these activities are to be found on the society's website, **www.blackcountrysociety.co.uk**, and in *The Blackcountryman*, the quarterly magazine that is distributed to all members.

*PO Box 71 · Kingswinford · West Midlands DY6 9YN*

# CONTENTS

Introduction 5

1 Setting Out From Wolverhampton 9

2 Bradley & Moxley 21

3 Darlaston & Pleck 25

4 Wednesbury 31

5 Walsall 43

6 Bloxwich 63

7 West Bromwich 69

8 Both Sides of the Stour (Cradley, Quarry Bank & Wollaston) 91

9 Gospel Halls 103

10 The Elim Churches 119

11 Bethels & the Assemblies of God 125

12 Independent Evangelical Churches 159

Acknowledgements 160

Throughout the time I have spent compiling this series of books, the chapel-related topic that most people have wanted to recall and discuss has been the business of Sunday School anniversaries. They form the most frequently photographed aspect of the chapel world. In some cases it is easier to locate an anniversary picture than to find a photograph of a particular building. Here we see a Sunday School anniversary pictured – the April 1956 anniversary at the Congregational Chapel in Oxford Street, Bilston. No usable picture of the exterior of this chapel has yet been found but Margaret Weston (née Chance), third from left on the back row, was able to provide this striking photograph. The chapel closed a few years later and the congregation moved to a temporary structure in Bunkers Hill Lane before moving into Portway Congregational Church.

# INTRODUCTION

This is the third of my books looking at the history of Black Country chapels. When work on the series began it seemed a good idea to compile a book illustrated with a representative selection of local chapels with the primary purpose of alerting readers to the fact that chapels seemed to be closing and that we ought to take a better look at them and recognise the amount of local heritage that has resided in them. My aim was to provide samples of different kinds of architecture, and show the vast range of human activity that has gone on in and around our chapels.

Since the publication of *Black Country Chapels* in 2004 the project has widened. Many people felt left out of the first volume and therefore it seemed a good idea to be slightly more comprehensive in my approach, rather than just representative. However, even with the publication of *More Black Country Chapels* in 2006, it was obvious that there were going to be large and important areas of the Black Country that were not being covered. That is why this volume has many chapters that are geographical. To most Methodists it will seem amazing that it has taken me three books to get round to looking at Wednesbury.

The other respect in which this project has widened as the books have progressed is in denominational terms. In the nineteenth century many chapels were built by the Baptists, Methodists and Congregationalists, plus a few Presbyterians and Unitarians, but in the twentieth century these mainstream non-conformists have been joined by a host of other denominations, some of whom see themselves as non-denominational. Some do in fact have roots stretching back into the nineteenth century, such as the Brethren. Others sprang up in response to a series of revivals and are still doing so today.

Recent years haven't just been about closures. There have been some spectacular openings and triumphant anniversaries. Here we see Norman Coley raising the flag outside the brand new Salvation Army Church in Meredith Street, Cradley Heath, on 13 August 2006. The official opening took place a month later on 9 September when Mrs Sylvia Heal MP cut the tape. *(NW)*

In the 1920s the Jeffreys bothers were instrumental in establishing the Elim Churches and the Assemblies of God. In 1930, Edward Jeffreys (the son of Stephen Jeffreys), established the Bethel Assemblies. In 1930 he conducted a crusade across the Black Country, which is described in Chapter 12. This resulted in the creation of a number of Bethel Temples, and inspired further expansion of the existing Pentecostal churches. Some Bethels later became aligned with the Assemblies of God and some became independent. This book only begins to grapple with the complexity of all this. Such institutions have often shown scant regard for preserving their own archives – perhaps caring for history is a rather worldly pursuit compared with the more urgent business of saving souls – but this book tries to include them, to make us all aware of their contribution to local non-conformity, and to encourage the newer churches to take their history seriously from now on.

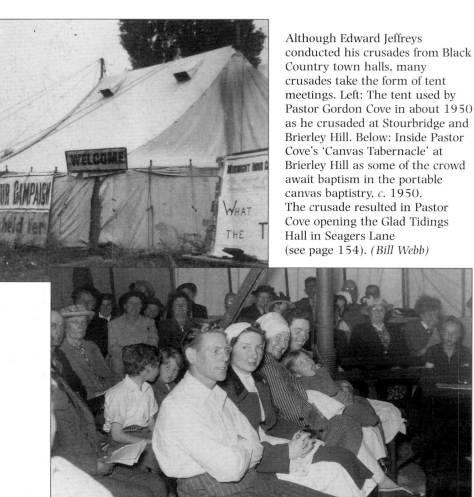

Although Edward Jeffreys conducted his crusades from Black Country town halls, many crusades take the form of tent meetings. Left: The tent used by Pastor Gordon Cove in about 1950 as he crusaded at Stourbridge and Brierley Hill. Below: Inside Pastor Cove's 'Canvas Tabernacle' at Brierley Hill as some of the crowd await baptism in the portable canvas baptistry, c. 1950. The crusade resulted in Pastor Cove opening the Glad Tidings Hall in Seagers Lane (see page 154). (Bill Webb)

Most churches and chapels have seen the provision and promotion of Sunday Schools as a high priority, hence the number of pictures of parades, anniversaries and other Sunday School activities.

The Sunday School at St John's Methodist Church, Wolverhampton, lines up to open in the new church on 19 August 1962. *(Peter Hickman/Graham Wycherley)*

The anniversary at Dale Street Methodist Church, Walsall, 1948. *(Alan Price)*

With the completion of the third book in this series most, but not all, areas of the Black Country have been covered, but some have been covered more comprehensively than others. With a closer look at the Gospel Halls of the Brethren and the survey of the assemblies that grew up after the Jeffreys' Crusade, a better denominational spread has been achieved. Even so, I know there are still many chapels not mentioned, and aspects of local Protestant non-conformity that have not been explored.

The conclusions to be drawn are that chapels are a major component in what we call local history, and that they have a complex history, sometimes resulting in closure and loss, but also often resulting in revival, renewal and reinvention. The problem is that we need to make sure that an adequate record is made of all this activity so that future generations can catch a glimpse of it.

Fund-raising is an essential part of chapel activity, from erecting buildings to the endless round of maintenance and improvement. Christmas bazaars, coffee mornings and summer fêtes all play their part. Here we see Sir Alfred Owen opening a bazaar at Dale Street Methodist Church, Walsall. (*Frank Preece*)

Many chapels include memorials to members of the congregation who died on war service. In this case Les Churm has provided a 'Prayer Card' – a card reminding the congregation to pray for an absent member – and in this case displayed at Leamore Methodist Church, Walsall, during the Second World War. (*Les Churm*)

# 1    Setting Out From Wolverhampton

A few of Wolverhampton's chapels were briefly described in *Black Country Chapels*, and many more were described in *More Black Country Chapels*. The area that has hardly been covered at all is the area to the south-east of the city centre from Blakenhall out to Parkfield and Lanesfield. In this chapter we begin by returning to Stratton Street because the chapel has recently celebrated a centenary and then begin the journey south-eastwards.

The Primitive Methodists laid the foundation stones of this chapel in Stratton Street, in the Park Village area of Wolverhampton, on 1 October 1906. This photograph was taken before the building was completed, but construction must have proceeded quickly as it was opened on 14 January 1907. (Compare this picture with the one on page 127 of *More Black Country Chapels*). The Stratton Street chapel partly replaced an earlier Primitive Methodist chapel which had existed in Culwell Street, just off the Cannock Road near Wolverhampton's Low Level station. A vestry was added in 1915, and a porch and entrance had been added by 1937. The porch contains a small table from Cross Street Chapel when the congregation from Heath Town merged with the folks here at Stratton Street in 1937. Sunday Schools and youth work prospered at Stratton Street and by the Second World War there was much talk of extending the premises by using the corner site just visible in the top picture. The construction of the hall began in 1957 and it was opened in 1965. Since then the chapel has played an increasing community role and facilities have gone through a number of improvements and reopenings. All this was celebrated in October 2006 when Stratton Street reached its centenary.

A 1950s Sunday School anniversary at Stratton Street. The scholars and leaders are lined up on the platform erected in front of the arch that still forms a distinctive feature of the front of the chapel. *(Stratton Street Centenary Archives)*

The 14th Wolverhampton Company of the Boys' Brigade was established at Stratton Street Methodist Chapel, and here we see something of the street itself as the boys line up for parade in the 1950s. The 1st Wolverhampton Company of the Girls' Life Brigade was also established at Stratton Street. *(Stratton Street Centenary Archives)*

White dresses are order of the day in Stratton Street as the girls of the Sunday School line up for a Sunday School Anniversary Parade in the 1920s. *(Stratton Street Centenary Archives)*

Taking a break from work on preparing the new church hall for its opening on 23 January 1965. Left to right: Jack Kerr, Brian Juggins, Arthur Jones, Ken Appleby, the Revd Jack Dowson and Ron Appleby. The Appleby family had come from Cross Street when that chapel closed in 1937. *(Stratton Street Centenary Archives)*

A portrait of the Stratton Street 'Family' taken at a harvest festival service, autumn 2001. Congregations are frequently full of people linked by family. In this picture there are a number of Jugginses and Manningses. At the same time as this picture was taken, the Methodist Conference was being held in Wolverhampton. *(Stratton Street Centenary Archives)*

The congregation assembled in the Stratton Street Chapel on 1 October 2006 for the centenary service. The Revd Inderjit Bhogal, past minister at Stratton Street, and past president of the Methodist Conference, takes a front seat on the right before the service begins. *(NW)*

The Revd Inderjit
Bhogal preaches at
the centenary
service at Stratton
Street on 1 October
2006. *(NW)*

The Revd Inderjit Bhogal, ex-Sunday
School scholar Anthony Tagg,
ex-minister the Revd Bryan Rippon and
the Revd Tony Kinch prepare to bless
and cut the centenary cake on 1 October
2006. *(NW)*

Angela Daniel (piano) and her son
Thomas (trumpet) play in memory of her
mother Joan Manning (née Juggins) who
played the piano at Stratton Street for
forty-seven years.

While Stratton Street has been celebrating its centenary the surviving Methodist chapels in Wolverhampton have been regrouping to form a city-based circuit of seven congregations. The Methodist Church in Low Hill closed on 8 May 2005 and was demolished soon afterwards after serving its community for over eighty years. *(NW)*

The Primitive Methodists established themselves in Lord Street, Wolverhampton, in 1833 and then expanded to other areas such as Blakenhall. Here in the Dudley road, on the corner with Derry Street, they built this chapel in about 1860, followed by a Sunday School in 1895. The church closed in 1956 when the roof became unsafe. The congregation transferred to Ranelagh Road and then St John's. *(Graham Wycherley Collection)*

The Wesleyan Methodists opened a chapel on the Dudley road, Blakenhall, at the end of the 1830s. By the 1870s they had outgrown the premises. The stone-laying for this replacement in Ranelagh Road took place on 2 November 1885, and it was opened on 17 May 1886, a Sunday School following in 1889. Having absorbed the congregation from Bethel, the eventual closure and sale of Ranelagh Road in about 1960 made a major contribution towards purchasing the land for the new church – St John's. *(Graham Wycherley Collection)*

The interior of the Ranelagh Road Chapel, showing the Nicholson organ which had been installed in 1910 at a cost of £350. *(Graham Wycherley Collection)*

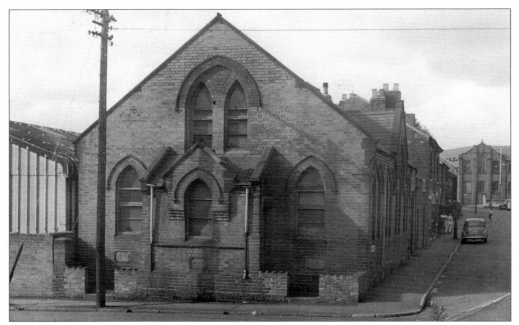

The Pountney Street Mission in Blakenhall was an early casualty – it closed in 1950. Ironically the building still survives in industrial use while the other chapels have disappeared. *(Graham Wycherley Collection)*

The old Methodist chapel at Parkfield was built in 1849, and was originally part of the Bilston circuit until 1916. It was on the southern side of Parkfield Road not far from the Fighting Cocks, and is not to be confused with the Primitive Methodist chapel in Parkfield Road, at the Ettingshall end, featured on page 56 of *Black Country Chapels*. *(Graham Wycherley Collection)*

In 1960 land was purchased at Parkfield Hall to replace the aging, or already abandoned Methodist chapels of Blakenhall and Parkfield. On 22 July 1961 three young ladies – each a representative of the Bethel, Ranelagh Road and Parkfield congregations – performed a turf-cutting ceremony. Left to right: Jane Hewitt, Joyce Cox and Norma Venables, watched by the Revd David Le Seelleur, Douglas Hartland, Fred Goodwill, the Revd John Jackson, and Mr James Warnock. *(Graham Wycherley Collection)*

On 16 August 1962 St John's Methodist Church, Parkfield, was opened in a series of ceremonies. Here we see the oldest trustees, Messrs Cresswell and Plant, unlocking the doors. *(Graham Wycherley Collection)*

St John's, Parkfield, was designed by Messrs Upright and Gallimore, and was built by Biddulph and Thrift at a cost of £42,000. Financial assistance came from the Joseph Rank Trust and a Miss Alice Onions of the Parkfield congregation who had died in 1956 and left money so that a new church could be built. *(Graham Wycherley Collection)*

On the day after the official opening of St John's Methodist Church, there was another ceremony (on Sunday 19 August 1962) to mark the opening of the Sunday School. Here we see Wilf Southall, the Sunday School Superintendent, leading the scholars into the new building at 2.45pm. That evening a farewell service for the minister, the Revd David Le Seelleur, who was leaving for Runcorn. *(Graham Wycherley Collection)*

The first Methodist chapel in Lanesfield, a village on the outskirts of Wolverhampton, was built in 1834, but was replaced by the one shown above in 1850. The Sunday School building seen on the right was built in 1909, replacing an earlier building from 1877. The village has gradually been swallowed by suburban housing and it was decided that this would be better served by building a new church on the other side of the Birmingham New Road. (*Robert Hampson Collection*)

The new Lanesfield Methodist Chapel was built in Laburnum Road and is seen here in 2006. It was opened on 16 December 1961 by Mrs David Lewis. A congregation from the Ladymoor Methodists joined Lanesfield at the end of 1975, bringing with them a clock that is now to be found in the entrance of this building. (*NW*)

A Sunday School anniversary picture taken at the old Lanesfield Chapel in Spring Road, early 1950s. *(Betty Hopkins)*

The Ladies' Fellowship at Lanesfield Methodist Church photographed beneath the Boys' Brigade shield in the Church Hall, 23 May 2006. The Boys' Brigade is still going strong at this chapel. *(NW)*

# 2    Bradley & Moxley

Leaving Wolverhampton via Lanesfield we come to Bradley, a village on the eastern side of Bilston. It was here that 'Iron-mad' Wilkinson was persuaded to build an iron chapel for the Methodists. The iron pulpit still survives. Moxley is a small village sandwiched between Bilston, Darlaston and Wednesbury.

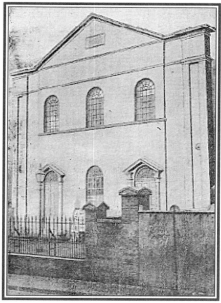

The first Wesleyan Methodist Chapel in Hall Green Street, Bradley, dated from 1835, and was built in the classical style. It was slightly rebuilt in 1899 but was then destroyed by fire in 1901, after being struck by lightning. The foundation stone for the replacement building, seen below, was laid on 21 April 1902 and it was opened later that year. The building was designed by C.W.D. Joynson, architect of a number of local chapels.

The second Wesleyan Methodist chapel in Hall Green Street, Bradley, was a typical turn-of-the-twentieth century building in brick and terracotta. It lasted until 1979 by which time the Methodist Chapels of Bradley had amalgamated, and a new modern church in Hall Green Street was subsequently built. (See page 106 of Ron Davies's *Bilston, Bradley & Ladymoor: A Fourth Selection*). Remains of the Sunday School building next door survive. (*Both Robert Hampson Collection*)

Moxley was created as an ecclesiastical parish of the Church of England in 1845, but Methodism was already strongly established in the area. Moxley became part of Darlaston UDC in 1894. The Bourne Primitive Methodist Chapel was erected in 1873 in the High Street. It took its name from one of the founders of Primitive Methodism, Hugh Bourne. Left to right: Cynthia Wilkes, Marjorie Lewis, Les Bagby, Mr Hinton, Mr Pooler, Mr Fellows, Arthur Felton, Ike Morris, Mrs Felton, Mrs Fellows, Charlie Moore, Bill Mills, Gladys Bailey and Christopher Lloyd. *(Cynthia Wilkes via Ian Bott)*

The 1911 Sunday School anniversary photograph was taken in the garden at the home of Mr William Wesson. The chapel at Moxley was greatly supported by the Wesson brothers who had bought the Victoria Ironworks at Moxley at the end of the nineteenth century, saving many local jobs. *(Keith Perry)*

A Sunday School anniversary at the Bourne Chapel, Moxley, 1953. The minister, Mr Brown, can be seen on the left. *(Cynthia Wilkes via Ian Bott)*

The Wesleyan Methodist Chapel was built in 1853 on the opposite side of the High Street to the Bourne Chapel, and is seen here in about 1900. Both chapels have now been replaced by the modern Methodist Centre. *(Jean Phillips via Ian Bott)*

A Sunday School anniversary picture taken at the Moxley Wesleyan Methodist Chapel in about 1957. *(David Phillips)*

Young and old at the new Methodist Centre in Moxley, which was opened in April 1983. Members of the congregation line up outside the new building in 2001. Far left is Brenda Evans, one of the stewards, and on the far right is Ian Southall, a local preacher. Next to Ian is the late Joe Phillips who, as a Sunday School teacher, was mentioned fifty-five years earlier in the Wesleyan chapel's centenary booklet! *(David Phillips)*

# 3    Darlaston & Pleck

Darlaston, once one of the most heavily industrialised towns of the Black Country, is associated with the early missions of the Primitive Methodists, walking from North Staffordshire to South Staffordshire to spread the word. However, the Wesleyan, New Connexion, and Wesleyan Reform arms of Methodism have also had a presence in the town. Our survey also spreads into Kings Hill in that area between Darlaston and Wednesbury, and into Pleck between Darlaston and Walsall.

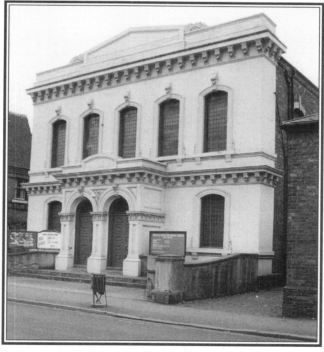

The Wesleyan Methodist Chapel in Pinfold Street dated from 1810. This picture, dating from September 1969, shows it in an enlarged and rebuilt form. The building was demolished in 1972 when the Methodists consolidated in Slater Street (the last service at Pinfold Street was in August 1971). Although no trace of the building is to be seen today and the site itself is obliterated by Lawrence Way, a short street close to the site of the burial ground is named Wesley Close. *(Alan Price)*

A Wesleyan Society was also established in Darlaston Green in the 1830s. The first chapel was built in 1844 in Horton Street but quickly suffered the effects of subsidence. The replacement, seen here in 1971, was built in 1870–1 alongside The Green. A wooden Sunday School building was added many years later in 1949, and was known locally as 'The Matchbox'. (See page 48 of *Black Country Chapels*). *(Keith Perry)*

The Primitive Methodists established their headquarters at Bell Street. The first chapel was built in 1836–7 but was much enlarged in 1879 in the form in which it is seen here. Subterranean fires in the coal measures caused its abandonment and the congregation moved to Slater Street. *(Keith Perry)*

*Above:* The 'new' Primitive Methodist chapel in Slater Street, much closer to the centre of Darlaston, opened on 14 April 1910. A Sunday School building was opened next door in 1912. It is the Sunday School building which is seen here, still surviving in 2006. The 1910 chapel building was replaced with a modern church centre which opened on 30 August 1980. *(NW)*

The Primitive Methodists also opened a chapel in Fallings Heath on the Walsall Road, opposite Cook Street. It was built in 1862, and closed in December 1968. This leaflet dates from 1913. *(Keith Perry Collection)*

The Methodist New Connexion also opened a chapel in Fallings Heath on the opposite side of the road, but no trace of either chapel remains.

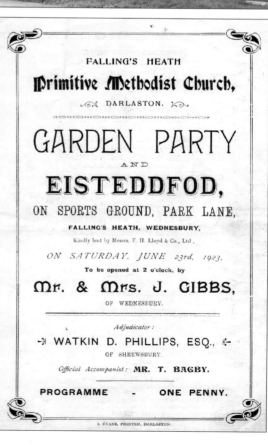

FALLING'S HEATH

**Primitive Methodist Church,**

DARLASTON.

# GARDEN PARTY

AND

# EISTEDDFOD,

ON SPORTS GROUND, PARK LANE,

FALLING'S HEATH, WEDNESBURY,

Kindly lent by Messrs. F. H. Lloyd & Co., Ltd ,

*ON SATURDAY, JUNE 23rd, 1923,*

To be opened at 2 o'clock, by

## Mr. & Mrs. J. GIBBS,

OF WEDNESBURY.

*Adjudicator :*

WATKIN D. PHILLIPS, ESQ.,

OF SHREWSBURY.

*Official Accompanist :* MR. T. BAGBY.

**PROGRAMME    -    ONE PENNY.**

J. EVANS, PRINTER, DARLASTON.

The Methodists of the New Connexion established themselves in Darlaston in 1852 with the building of this chapel, built in the 'V' of Great Croft Street. It was already abandoned when it was photographed on 1 September 1969. *(Alan Price)*

Kings Hill feels like a suburb of Darlaston although it is technically in Wednesbury. The Wesleyan Methodists built a chapel, tucked away at the end of Chapel Lane, in 1839 and enlarged it a year later. The congregation again outgrew it and moved to a new chapel in 1857, selling the old one to the Primitive Methodists. The Primitive Methodists also prospered and built this new chapel, opened in January 1909. A memorial window featured the founders of Primitive Methodism, and the chapel was sometimes known as the Centenary Chapel as its opening coincided with the centenary of the founding of the denomination. This contemporary postcard view was sold by B.D. Smith, newsagent of Walsall Road, Wednesbury. *(Ian Bott Collection)*

The Salvation Army was established in Darlaston by two female officers: Captain Nellie Moore and Lt Angela Reynolds. The first 'barracks' were in Cock Street, formerly the Temperance Hall. By the time this picture was taken in about 1973, Cock Street was known as High Street, and the hall was about to be demolished to make way for an Asda store. The hall at The Leys dates from 20 September 1975 when opened by Lt-Col. Frank Powell. *(Bev Parker)*

A presentation taking place in the Salvation Army building in the 1960s. Major Richardson, Divisional Youth Secretary (left), presents Sue Pearce with a singing leader's certificate, watched by Capt and Mrs Tite, among others. *(Bev Parker)*

Pleck is a small village between Darlaston and Walsall. Methodism has a history in Pleck going back to cottage meetings that began in 1827. In 1840 they opened their first chapel in St Quentin Street, then named Chapel Street. They outgrew this building and purchased land in Regent Street, now known as Caledon Road, to build a fine new chapel. This was opened on 26 August 1861. A Sunday School building was added in 1865.

On 20 February 1899 a meeting was held at The Grange, Bescot, the home of Enoch Horton, a local county councillor and magistrate. He wanted to build a much larger chapel at Pleck. A site was purchased on the corner of Bescot Road and Wednesbury Road and C.W.D. Joynson drew up the plans for a chapel to accommodate over 700 people. Mr Lees, the Darlaston building contractor, built the chapel for £5,000.

Here we see Enoch Horton on the extreme right witnessing the stonelaying at Pleck on 16 August 1899. The chapel, seen left, was opened on 15 January 1901 by Horton. A Nicholson organ was added in 1903 in memory of the late Mrs Horton and a Sunday school building was added in 1915.

The old chapel in Caledon Street was sold to the Primitive Methodists, although, of course, many years later the congregations amalgamated. Enoch Horton's grand chapel was demolished and a small modern chapel was built integrated into some flats provided for senior citizens. *(Barbara Lowe)*

# 4    Wednesbury

The physical landscape of Wednesbury is dominated by the hill-top presence of the Anglican parish church and the nearby Roman Catholic church. The religious history of Wednesbury is dominated by John Wesley.

Charles Wesley visited Wednesbury in 1742 and the congregation, or 'society', that then formed invited John Wesley in 1743. In all, John Wesley visited Wednesbury over thirty times. On a number of occasions he preached from the famous 'horse block' – a flight of stone steps adjoining a building in High Bullen. These steps are preserved today in Wednesbury's modern Methodist Centre. Many of Wesley's visits and the resulting spread of Methodism provoked riots and vicious attacks on Methodist supporters. One of John Wesley's last visits – in March 1788 when he was eighty-seven years old – was in the local society's meeting house and he was able was able to feel satisfied that God's work was finally being accomplished in the town. This first Wesleyan meeting house had been built in 1760 in what became known as Meeting Street. The building remained in use until 1813, when the Methodists moved to Spring Head.

Non-conformity flourished in Wednesbury in the 1760s as the Independent Dissenters (later known as Congregationalists) also built their first chapel in 1762. The building that became the Baptist chapel in Holyhead Road is now a tyre-fitting centre. Congregationalism's most prominent contribution to the stock of Wednesbury's non-conformist chapels was made in 1905 with the opening of Trinity on the Walsall Road.

In 1824 the Primitive Methodists opened their first chapel in Wednesbury in Camp Street. Through the nineteenth and twentieth centuries the story of Wednesbury's chapels becomes quite tortuous, and the town seems to have possessed an unusually high number of buildings which enjoyed changes of denominational ownership. Let's hope this can be made clear.

The steps on which Wesley stood to preach in Wednesbury are preserved in the Methodist's Wesley Centre in Spring Head, seen here in 2006. They originally gave access to a malthouse in High Bullen from which they were first moved in 1891. (NW)

A Baptist chapel was built in Dudley Street, Wednesbury in 1838, but ten years later the congregation had moved to this building in Holyhead Road. A Sunday School building was added at the rear in 1881–2. The Baptists moved again in 1961 and are now to be found in the ex-Methodist chapel in Vicar Street. This picture was taken in 1968 when the chapel was empty. It was bought by a tyre-fitting company and is still used for that purpose today. *(Alan Price)*

The Baptist Sunday School building, seen from Stafford Street, still stands in 2007. It carries a plaque telling us that the foundation stone was laid on 3 October 1881 and that it was opened on 22 January 1882. (Note the rear of the chapel on the right). *(NW)*

An 'Independent' congregation of eighteenth-century Dissenters built the chapel in Holyhead Road (pictured on the opposite page) in the 1760s. It was rebuilt in 1831 and then sold to the Baptists in 1848. The 'Independents' then built this chapel in Russell Street. It is built of Peldon stone a coal measures sandstone quarried locally at the Monway Field, and was completed by 1850. By the beginning of the twentieth century they described themselves as Congregationalists and moved once again to Walsall Street (see below). At one stage a corrugated iron building was added to the complex, but this was later sold to a congregation in Liverpool. In 1905 the Russell Street building was sold to the Parish of St John to become their 'Institute'. St John's itself was demolished in 1985 and the 'Institute' has now become a Masonic Hall. *(NW)*

Trinity was built by Wednesbury's Congregationalists in Walsall Street in 1904 at a cost of £4,300 with the intention of being able to accommodate up to 600 people. It was the first church in Wednesbury to be lit by electricity, and was designed by C.W.D. Joynson, built by the Hammond brothers and was opened on 10 January 1905. Despite such optimism the congregation has not survived and the building is now a Muslim Centre. Its red brick and terracotta frontage has now been painted white which has rather dramatically changed the cosmetic appearance of the building. *(Ian Bott)*

As mentioned on page 31, Wednesbury was much visited by John Wesley and it is not surprising that eventually Methodism took a strong hold on the town. The Anti-Wesley 'riot' of 20 October 1743 is commemorated in this picture by Marshall Claxton. A copy hangs in the Wesley Centre to this day. Wesley was confronted by the mob and taken off to face magistrates at Bentley Hall and Walsall. At neither place would the magistrates take any action against Wesley. He eventually escaped when the Wednesbury mob tangled with their counterparts at Walsall! *(Wesley Centre Archives)*

The Methodists eventually built a chapel at Spring Head. It was opened on 16 May 1813 and was originally lit by candles (gas lighting was introduced in 1828). The building was demolished in 1866 to make way for the new Spring Head Chapel. This photograph was taken by the minister, the Revd John Relf the day before demolition began. The site is now a car park. *(Wesley Centre Archives)*

The second (1867) Wesleyan Methodist Chapel at Spring Head was a very impressive and 'solid' building. It opened on 12 November 1867 and closed on 24 April 1932 in order to be rebuilt with a new modern frontage. *(Wesley Centre Archive)*

In 1932 a new frontage was built on to the 1867 chapel and the chapel became a Central Mission. Foundation stones had been laid on 23 July and it opened in its new guise on 31 October. (These events ran parallel to similar events at Ablewell Street Walsall.) It was finally demolished in 1965. *(Wesley Centre Archive)*

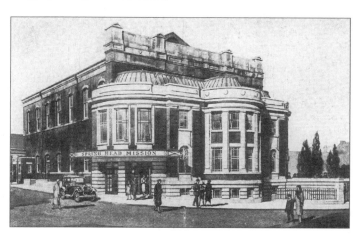

A substantial Wesleyan school building was built on the other side of Spring Head in the 1860s. It managed to survive until 1995 when it was finally demolished to provide space to build the new Wesley Centre. This photograph was taken just before demolition. *(Judith Wilson)*

The interior of the 1867 Spring Head Chapel, built by Trow and Sons, and designed by S. and J. Loxton. This interior was also rebuilt during the 1932 modernisation (see picture on page 37). *(Wesley Centre Archive)*

Huge crowds fill the road to see the opening of the rebuilt Wesleyan Chapel in Spring Head in October 1932. The new frontage managed to give the Victorian building a rather modern cinema-like entrance. *(Wesley Centre Archives)*

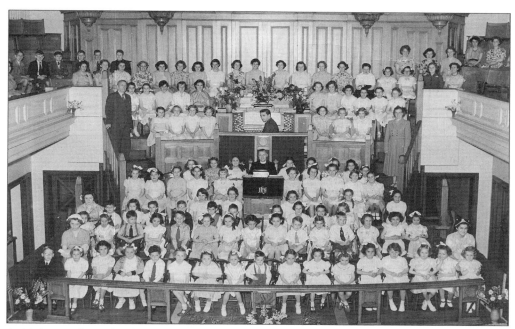

A 1953 Sunday School anniversary picture at Spring Head shows the degree to which the interior was modernised in the 1932 rebuild. The minister in the centre of the picture is the Revd Eric Bilton, and the organist is Ron Foster. The Sunday School superintendents, standing left and right, are John Ellis and Marie Hancox. *(Wesley Centre Archives)*

On 9 March 1968 the Revd Joe Henderson leads the opening party through the doors of the new building, watched by crowds in the road itself. *(Wesley Centre Archives)*

The first Sunday School anniversary to be held in the new chapel was held in June 1968, using a new platform. *(Wesley Centre Archives)*

One would expect a large anniversary in a chapel claiming to be a 'Central Mission', and of course it was the centre of many other activities, a point represented by this pantomime picture from the 1950s. The show was *Robin Hood*, and included in the picture are Alan Maybury, Herman Berry, Frank Phipps, Ted Evans, Hilda Hazel, Wilf Hancock, Carol Stevenson, Marion Evans, Bert Middleton and Janet Hancock. *(Wesley Centre Archives)*

The 1868/rebuilt 1932 Wesleyan Methodist chapel at Spring Head has now been replaced with the Wesley Centre. The church portion of this complex was opened on 9 March 1968. The old school building was demolished in the 1990s to make way for the transformation and extension (seen on the right) of the 1968 church into the Wesley Centre, which opened on 28 September 1996. *(NW)*

Leigh Maydew, Margaret Haden, Ann Thomson and daughter Esther display Boys' Brigade and Girl Guide standards kept at the centre, and Margaret's models of the churches which had come together to form the present congregation. *(NW)*

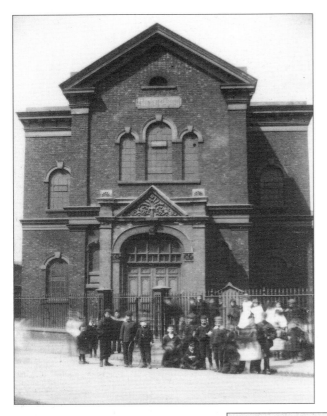

The Wesley Methodist Chapel in Holyhead Road, Wednesbury, was opened in 1850, and was enlarged in 1893 to accommodate 600 people at a cost of £1,000. It was at that time that it acquired the frontage seen here in the 1900s. It gained some importance as the centre of a circuit that took in chapels in Hill Top, Great Bridge, Gospel Oak, Toll End and Swan Village. It closed in 1957 and was demolished while the congregation moved to Spring Head.

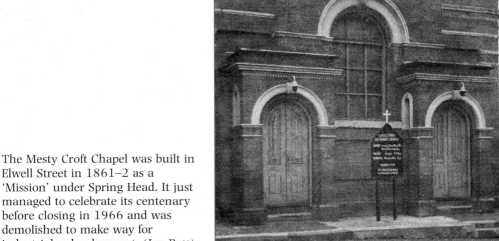

The Mesty Croft Chapel was built in Elwell Street in 1861–2 as a 'Mission' under Spring Head. It just managed to celebrate its centenary before closing in 1966 and was demolished to make way for industrial redevelopment. *(Ian Bott)*

The Primitive Methodists established themselves at Camp Street, opening this chapel as early as 14 November 1824. The last service was held at Camp Street on 26 June 1966 and the building was demolished in 1970 to clear the site for the relocation of Wednesbury Market. *(Wesley Centre Archives)*

The Primitive Methodists built another chapel in Wednesbury in Vicarage Road in 1865, replaced by this magnificent chapel in Vicar Street. The foundation stones were laid on 11 May 1912 and it was opened on 14 November of the same year. It was designed by Messrs Scott and Clark, and was intended to accommodate 300 people. In the 1960s restructuring of the Methodist churches of Wednesbury, this building was sold to the Baptists who moved in during 1961. *(NW)*

The 1960s reorganisation of Methodism in Wednesbury resulted in the closure of five churches (Spring Head Mission, Vicar Street, Elwell Street, Ridding Lane and Camp Street) and the building of two new ones: the Wesley Centre, and this building in Coronation Road on the Woods Estate. Woods Methodist Church was opened on 2 July 1966 by the Revd Gordon Wilson. The building seen here was intended to be the church hall, but the church 'proper' has still not been built. Recent modifications to the interior have made it a good multi-use centre. *(Judith Wilson)*

The Methodist Chapel in Ridding Lane was opened in 1866 by the Methodist New Connexion. The balcony collapsed two years later during an anti-Irish lecture and the front of the building was remodelled late in the nineteenth century when it became the United Methodist Free Church. Since the 1960s the congregation has been absorbed by the Wesley Centre, and after use as a clothing warehouse it has been demolished. *(Ian Bott)*

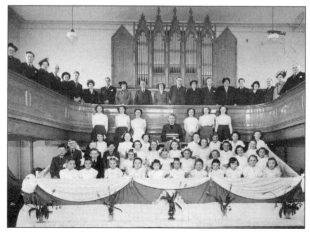

Happier times at Ridding Lane – a Sunday School anniversary in the 1950s. *(Ian Bott)*

# 5    Walsall

Walsall dominates the north-eastern quarter of the Black Country and has been the centre of a great deal of non-conformist activity. The Baptists, the 'Independents', and the Methodists have all built a number of chapels, not forgetting the Apostolic and Pentecostal assemblies and fellowships who are dealt with later in this book. It is interesting to note that Edward Jeffreys chose Walsall as the starting point of his Black Country crusade of 1930, and that created a number of congregations in its wake.

Baptists can trace their presence in Walsall back to the mid-seventeenth century. A group of Baptists meeting in the assembly room at the Black Boy in the 1830s decided to build this chapel in Goodhall Street in 1833. The drawing dates from the 1880s, after which the front of the building was modified. The foundation stone was laid on 7 April 1833 and it was opened on 23 September the following year. It was just 40ft square and had cost £650 to build. The later Baptist churches in the area often developed from the work of people from Goodhall Street. (*Walsall Local History Centre*)

A section of the Goodhall Street Baptist congregation succeeded in the 1840s and built their own chapel, known as the Ebenezer, in Stafford Street in 1846–7. Opened on 25 January 1847, it was enlarged in 1869 and the classical façade seen in this picture was added. It ceased to be used by the Baptists on 30 September 1972 and the congregation moved to the new Baptist Chapel in Green Lane. (*NW*)

Baptists from Ebenezer (Stafford Street) planted this chapel in Vicarage Walk, Caldmore, in 1879. It was still being used by the Baptists when this picture was taken in August 1969, but closed in 1985. The building has survived and is now used by the Sikh community. *(Alan Price)*

A group of Particular Baptists was established in Walsall in 1840, led by George Nicklin. In 1845 they were able to acquire a vacant Primitive Methodist chapel in Newport Street and Lower Hall Lane in which they stayed until moving to this new building in Midland Road. It was opened on Tuesday 24 March 1910, and teas were provided in the Masonic Hall in the High Street. Since its closure a factory has obliterated the site. *(Len Burrows)*

The Congregationalists built this chapel in Bridge Street in 1838 in which a key figure was the father of the famous writer Jerome K. Jerome. The Bridge Street Chapel was later rebuilt in the form seen below. *(Walsall Local History Centre)*

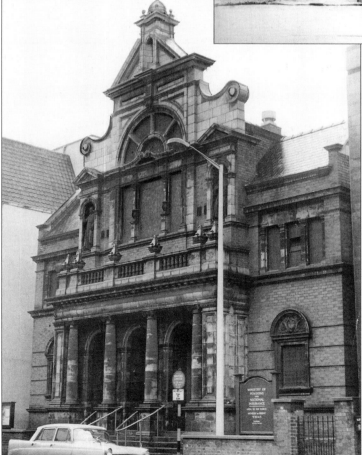

*Left:* The huge Congregational Chapel in Bridge Street became redundant when the church on the Broadway was opened in 1958. The photograph was taken in March 1964 while the building was being used by the Ministry of Pensions. *(Express & Star)*

Another group of Congregationalists took over an old Free Methodist Chapel in Blakenhall Lane (at the junction of Booth Street) in 1882. They eventually built a very modern chapel at the junction of Blakenhall Lane and Chantry Avenue in 1936, but that has now been replaced by new building.

The Congregationalists built this chapel in Mill Street, Ryecroft, in 1860, reflecting their policy of establishing themselves in the town centre and then planting churches in the working-class suburbs. This policy is also seen at work in Wolverhampton and Dudley. Mill Street is seen here in 2006 occupied by the Church of God. The building is currently used by the Seventh Day Adventists. *(NW)*

Jerome K. Jerome's father was among a number of Congregationalists who decided to leave Bridge Street and build this chapel, which he had designed, in Wednesbury Road. It opened in 1860 and later acquired some fame during the First World War when it survived a Zeppelin raid. Demolition finally came in 1974 by which time the congregation had joined their colleagues from Bridge Street in creating a United Reformed congregation in The Broadway. The Glebe Centre now stands on part of the site. *(Alan Price)*

A new Congregational Church was built on The Broadway, which since 1972 has been a United Reformed Church. It was built with funds collected from the sale of the Bridge Street Chapel although construction did not start until 1958. It was opened by Dr Berry on 27 September 1959. *(NW)*

The Presbyterians in Walsall trace their ancestry back to an 'Independent congregation of Dissenters who had a meeting house in Bank Court, near the High Street in the seventeenth century. It was burned down in 1715 and was subsequently rebuilt. Although the congregation was small in number, they were augmented in 1876 by a group of defectors from the Bridge Street Congregationalists. A new chapel, seen here in 1969, was built in 1881–2 in Hatherton Street. It was designed by Messrs Cotton and McConnal in a semi-Gothic style. Since 1972 it has been known as the Hatherton United Reform Church. *(Alan Price)*

Some of the Presbyterians at the Bank Court Meeting House turned to Unitarianism and built Christ's Chapel in Stafford Street in 1827. It was a small brick building with a stuccoed façade. It is seen here on 2 August 1968, looking rather the worse for wear. *(Alan Price)*

The Baptists at Goodhall Street established several other Baptist chapels. This one, seen here in 2007, was set up on the corner of Lumley Street and The Crescent in 1919. *(NW)*

## Methodism in Walsall

John Wesley's first visit to Walsall was on the night of 20 October 1743 and was a result of being captured by a mob in Wednesbury and then snatched by a mob from Walsall, from whom he escaped. His second visit was twenty years later and the welcome given to him by a large number of people led him to remark, 'How is Walsall changed!'

A Methodist Society was immediately formed as a result of the second visit, at first meeting in a house in New Street, then moving to Dudley Street in 1770. 'Upper rooms' were later used at the Castle Inn and then the White Lion Inn. At the latter the first Methodist Chapel was built in the early 1800s, known to all as 'Bedlam'.

From 'Bedlam' the Wesleyan Methodists planned and then built the first chapel in Ablewell Street in 1828, followed by the Centenary Chapel in Stafford Street in 1840.

The Wesley Methodist Chapel built in Ablewell Street in 1828 was regarded as one of the best buildings of its kind in the Midlands. A house was built next door to accommodate the minister, and a Sunday School was built beneath it. A vestry and extra school room were added in 1834, the first of many alterations, additions and rebuilding programmes to take place on the site. The building is seen to the left of the picture. On the right is the 'Second Wesley', built in 1859 to accommodate up to 1,700 people. With the opening of the 1859 building on 3 November, the former chapel became a two-storey school building (both day school and Sunday School). The school building was finally closed and demolished in 1959 to make way for the Community Hall. (*Florence Harper Collection*)

The interior of the 1859 building looking towards the entrance in Ablewell Street. This arrangement meant that late-comers were visible to the entire congregation. The Nicholson organ seen here was added in 1860. A gallery ran round all four sides of the hall with the portion in front of the organ being used to house the choir.

On the opposite page it is possible to see the Nicholson organ of 1930 which dominated the end wall of the Central Mission in Ablewell Street. The organ was put in place on 4 January 1930 when a special recital was given by T.W. North, the borough organist, and Joseph Yates, vocalist and musical director of the mission. Note that the organ console faces the choir stalls making it possible for the organist to conduct the choir.

In 1929 the Wesley (Mark 2) Chapel in Ablewell Street was reconstructed at a cost of £26,000. The foundation stone was laid on 20 June 1929. The most obvious alteration was the addition of a new frontage, filling the space between the 1859 building and the line of the former railings. This was reopened as the Central Mission on Thursday 30 January 1930. Mrs S.M. Davis Green opened the hall, and when the new Community Hall was opened in 1961 a room was named after her. The hall proved too large in recent times and was divided in the early 1970s – the worship space being on the upper floor. Further changes were made in 2000. (*Florence Harper Collection*)

The Sunday School anniversary at Walsall Central, Ablewell Street, 1958. The party are seen in front of the new Nicholson organ installed in 1930. *(Florence Harper Collection)*

The Community Hall seen here next door to the Central Mission in 2006, was opened on 21 January 1961. *(NW)*

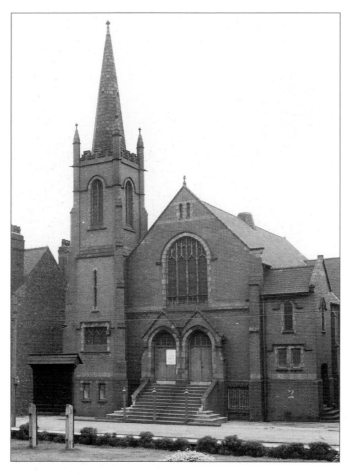

From their base in Ablewell Street, the Walsall Wesleyan Methodists supported the development of a number of new congregations. A Sunday School was opened in Stafford Street in 1839 while this chapel was being built for an opening in 1840. It took the name Centenary Chapel and in 1863 it became the head of a second Walsall circuit. It was enlarged several times, particularly in 1889, and was photographed here in 1969. *(Alan Price)*

In 1875 several trustees were elected at Ablewell Street and given the task of developing a new chapel on the Lichfield road, at the junction with Mellish Road, which they hoped would be a prosperous suburb of Walsall. Progress was slow and in 1881 a temporary second-hand 'tin chapel' was sought. One was not opened at Mellish Road until 5 June 1883.

The foundation stone for this building at Mellish Road was laid on 16 September 1909, and it opened on 24 September 1910. It was designed by Messrs Hickton and Farmer, and built by Messrs Streather and Hill. Sunday School buildings were added in 1935.

Inside Mellish Road Methodist Church, 18 September 1954. This is the wedding of Betty Walters and Ron Guy. The Revd Hodges conducted the ceremony and Anthony Harvey is playing the organ. *(Betty Guy Collection)*

*Wives Go West*, a drama production presented by the Wives' Fellowship at Mellish Road on 11 November 1965, directed by Alan Shorthouse. One night for the fellowship, one night for rehearsals, one night for the Drama Society – it was 'all go' at Mellish Road. *(Betty Guy Collection)*

Mellish Road Methodist Church Sisterhood's annual coach outing, 1953. The coach driver was not a member of the sisterhood but insisted in being in the picture! The group met on Monday afternoons, and the Wives' Fellowship on Monday evenings. On the left of the front row was Mrs Potts, the church caretaker's wife. *(Betty Guy Collection)*

The primary or younger members of the Mellish Road Sunday School and their teachers at an afternoon mini-version of the anniversary, 1962. The morning and evening services were packed for the full version of the Sunday School anniversary which was always a big occasion at Mellish Road, under the direction of the choirmaster, Mr Lakin-Smith. *(Betty Guy Collection)*

Releasing children from poverty
**Compassion**®
in Jesus' name

*A new photo of your sponsored child*

# AJIT

## INFORMATION ABOUT...

# AJIT

**BIRTHDAY**      18 December 1997
**COUNTRY**      India
**CHILD NO**      IN5120757

Ajit lives under the care of his parents. His home duties include running errands, carrying water and buying or selling in the market. There are 3 children in the family. His father is at times employed and his mother looks after the home.

For fun Ajit likes playing with friends, playing football, bicycling, playing marbles, playing with toy cars, reading, playing ping pong and playing ball games. He attends Sunday School & Church and Vacation Bible School regularly. He attends school where his performance is Average.

Please remember Ajit in your prayers. Your love and support will help him to receive the assistance he needs to grow and develop.

PROJECT: Andrews Kirk Child Development Center
LOCATION: Central Chennai

Project: IN-512, Andrews Kirk Child Development Centre
Location: SM Nagar, Chennai, India
Your sponsored child lives on the plains of SM Nagar, home to approximately 26,000 residents. Typical houses are constructed of dirt floors, adobe walls and thatch roofs. The primary ethnic group is Dravidian and the most commonly spoken language is Tamil.
The regional diet consists of bananas, fish and rice. Common health problems in this area include throat infections, tuberculosis, boils, anemia, malaria, fevers, vitamin deficiencies and dysentery. Most adults are unemployed but some work as day labourers and earn the equivalent of £25 per month. This community needs proper sanitation, employment opportunities and educational resources.
Your sponsorship allows the staff of Andrews Kirk Child Development Centre to provide your sponsored child with Bible teaching, nutritious food, hygiene supplies, medical checkups, literacy training, HIV/AIDS awareness programs, tutoring and recreational activities. The centre staff will also provide meetings and spiritual retreats for the parents or guardians of your sponsored child.

**Why not take a moment to write a short message to Ajit on the attached letter paper. Simply tear along the perforation and post to Compassion UK in the freepost envelope provided.**

Another Wesleyan Methodist congregation was established in Caldmore in 1876 and in the following year Trinity Chapel was built, designed in the Gothic style by Samuel Loxton. The Sunday School built at the rear of Trinity still survives and is used by a Pentecostal group. Trinity itself was demolished in the mid-1950s and the new building seen here was built 1957–8. A congregation from a Victor Street chapel joined the Trinity congregation, and now they are known as Caldmore Methodist Church. *(Walsall LHS)*

The present-day Caldmore Methodist Church with the remains of Trinity's Sunday School building behind it. *(NW)*

At Leamore, on the road out to Bloxwich, the Wesleyan Methodists built a chapel in 1862–3. This was compulsorily purchased by the council a hundred years later and a modern replacement was built on the corner of Carl Street (see overleaf). Another Wesleyan chapel was built on the corner of Bridgeman Street and Queen Street in 1867 and this was subsequently sold to the Bethel Movement (see pages 148 and 149).

This very modern chapel was built on the Bloxwich road on the corner of Carl Street, Leamore, to replace the Wesleyan chapel seen on the previous page. It was designed by J.M. Warnick, opened in 1965, and is seen here in 1969. The congregation from the former Primitive Methodist chapel joined the folks here but the numbers declined and the chapel was closed. It is now an antiques centre. *(Alan Price)*

The Wesleyans were also active in the Palfrey area of Walsall. A Palfrey Chapel in Dale Street was built in 1863, but it was replaced with this building, designed by Messrs Hicton and Farmer, which opened on 17 February 1910. This picture was taken in 1969. (*Alan Price*)

It seems likely that no picture of the original Dale Street chapel as built in 1863 survives, as it was replaced in 1909–10 with the building seen above. However this picture does survive, showing the 1887 Sunday School building. It was built in two months at a cost of £282. (*Frank Preece Collection*)

Like so many chapels, Dale Street once had a thriving youth club. Here are some of the members on the Delves Playing Field, *c.* 1950. Back row, left to right: Clarence Bassett, Jack Thompson, Frank Preece, Philip Greystone, -?-, Graham Cook, -?-. Second and third from left on the front row are Peter Long and Brian Hackworth. (*Frank Preece Collection*)

In February 1960 the Dale Street Methodists were celebrating the fiftieth anniversary of being in the 1910 building. The Revd Edgar Noble and his wife prepare to cut the cake. On the left is Cllr Greystone and on the extreme right it is just possible to see Billy Ellis, a veteran both of the congregation and of the Boer War! The congregation at Dale Street eventually declined and the chapel closed in November 1975. *(Frank Preece Collection)*

An anniversary picture from Dale Street dating from the early 1960s. At the front are Mrs Ann Huskison, who trained the children and the Revd Brian O'Gorman. *(Frank Preece Collection)*

The first Wesleyan Methodist chapel in Coalpool, way out on the eastern flanks of Walsall, was provided in 1852, but was replaced with this building in 1896. It is seen here in 2006. (NW)

The interior of the Coalpool Wesleyan Methodist Chapel, Coalpool Lane, 2006. The 110-year-old building now has bright decor and modern seating. (John James)

On 29 October 2006 the congregation at the Coalpool Methodist Chapel celebrated the 110th birthday of their building. The Revd Neville Ashton and his wife Margaret were invited to conduct the service. Neville had been minister at the chapel from 1991 to 1994. Also in the group is senior steward, Gordon Rowley. (John James)

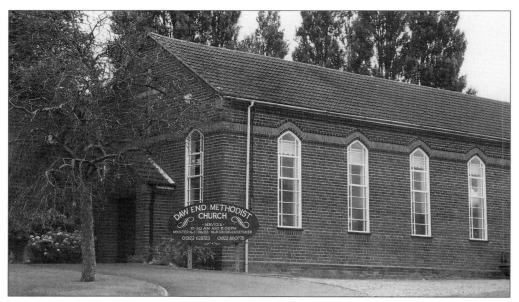

A small Methodist Society seems to have existed at Daw End since 1818, but a chapel did not materialise until 1903 when the Wesleyan Methodists bought a disused mission church in Floyds Lane. They nicknamed the modest building 'The Cathedral'. Interest from Central created a revival in the 1930s and plans were made for a new church on the present site. The war intervened and it was 1947 before even a Nissen hut with a brick frontage could be provided. This was finally replaced with the building seen here, which was opened on 19 March 1960. A Sunday School building was added in 1966.

Reedsworth Methodist Church, seen here in 2006, is home to a congregation created from the merger of two former chapels. The original chapel building on the right-hand side of this picture was the Pargeter Street chapel of 1902. In 1946 they were joined by the folks from Dalkeith Road chapel, Birchills, which had been destroyed by a fire on 23 August 1945 – possibly ignited by a spark from a bonfire lit to celebrate the end of the war! *(NW)*

The church and congregation at Reedswood Methodist Church, 1993. The building was about to go through a major refurbishment. *(Jo Kelford)*

Modern requirements include things like ramps for wheelchair access. This picture taken on 1 July 1995, shows the new ramp, the youth club building and the Revd Nichola Jones flanked by youngest and oldest members of the congregation. Although Reedswood has maintained a small Sunday School it held its last anniversary procession in June 2002. *(Jo Kelford)*

## The Primitive Methodists in Walsall

As we have seen the Wesleyan Methodists very successfully established themselves across Walsall and in the surrounding area. The Primitive Methodists are not so strongly represented. They first met in a room in George Street and then built a chapel on the corner of Lower Hall Lane and Newport Street in 1832–3. This was sold to the Strict and Particular Baptists (see page 44) and the Prims moved to the Ragged School at Townend Bank. In 1876 they opened Mount Zion on the corner of Blue Lane West and Margaret Street, but even this has now disappeared, having closed during the 1960s. It was subsequently demolished.

In Caldmore the Primitive Methodists built the Victor Street chapel in 1884, but this was closed in 1957 when they joined the Corporation Street (Trinity) congregation. The building was sold to the Jehovah's Witnesses in 1958. In Ryecroft they built a small chapel in North Street and then between 1900 and 1905 moved to a chapel in Stafford Street. The latter was closed in the mid-1960s and was later used as a warehouse.

As mentioned elsewhere, the Primitive Methodists had a presence in Pleck and Fallings Heath, and at Pinfold Street, Bloxwich, but once again we have to report that all these chapels have disappeared.

The Brethren and the post-1930 Pentecostal churches are also represented in Walsall, and in the case of the Stephenson Hall, on the Beechdale Estate, their paths cross. The tale begins as part of the Brethren story (see pages 103–18) when Frank Bissell, who had grown up as a member of the Wellcroft Street Assembly (see page 107), became involved in building the Beechdale Estate. He built the hall, as seen above, and it was opened on 7 June 1958. A decline began in the early 1960s and Frank Bissell approached Keith Tanner of the Regent Street 'temple' (see page 149) to see if he could take over the hall's work. It reopened as the Beechdale Evangelical Church on 15 March 1964. More recently the congregation has been rebadged as the Walsall Independent Evangelical Church and has moved back to a town-centre location at Bath Street (see page 149). Their last service here was held on 31 August 1997. (WIEC)

# 6    Bloxwich

The village of Bloxwich, in the north-eastern corner of the Black Country has been host to three Methodist congregations, one of each major persuasion, and an interesting gospel hall. The Congregationalists, meanwhile, have been served by a church in nearby Blakenhall.

During John Wesley's lifetime a Methodist Society was formed in Bloxwich and a small meeting house was built in Bullock's Fold in 1780–1. No trace of this remains as the works of Messrs S. Wilkes and Sons was later built on the site. It was replaced in 1832 with the Wesleyan Chapel in Park Road. It was enlarged by the addition of a Sunday School building on the back in 1856. The building later became known as the Central Hall and after the Methodists left it in 1864 they retained it as a Sunday School until 1910. It then saw a variety of uses including a short life as a cinema where the Wilkes family, Thomas Wood and Pat Collins all took turns at showing films. In 1937 Pat Collins sold the building, in which he had been repairing fairground equipment, to Bert Britain who used it as a garage. Interestingly the building survives today, and the chapel frontage illustrated above is still recognisable. *(Derek Fellows Collection)*

In the 1920s, the Wesleyan Methodist Church at Bloxwich produced a troupe of Pierrot singers and dancers. *(Derek Fellows Collection)*

In 1864 the building of a much bigger Wesleyan chapel began closer to the centre of Bloxwich. It opened on 28 August 1865, later becoming known as 'Wesley'. Using land in Victoria Road, 'Wesley' gradually expanded. A new Sunday School was built in 1910 to replace the Park Street premises, and in 1921 institute facilities were added, plus a caretaker's house in 1924. Tennis courts and a bowling green were added in 1926. Here we see Wesley with the posters outside announcing its closure in 1963.
(*Derek Fellows Collection*)

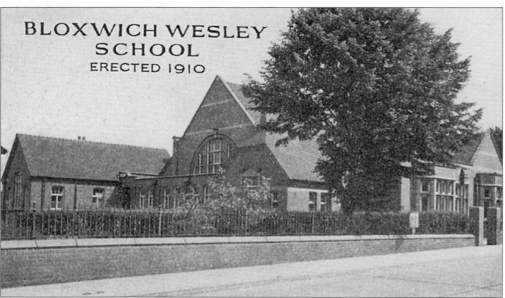

The Sunday School building of 1910, in Victoria Road.

A handbill survives which advertises the opening of the 1865 Wesleyan Chapel in Bloxwich. Note that 'Tea will be provided for friends coming from a distance'. Does that mean that local supporters were not given tea? The Revd Bambridge was minister for the first two years. *(Derek Fellows Collection)*

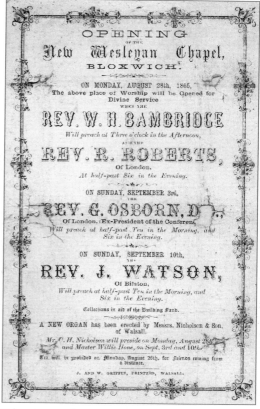

The interior of 'Wesley' is seen at the other end of the chapel's life. The photograph was taken just before closure in 1963. *(Derek Fellows Collection)*

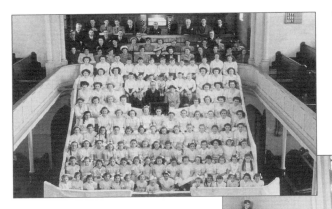

The vast platform of the Sunday School anniversary at the Wesleyan Chapel in Bloxwich on 16 May 1948. When compared with the picture below it can be seen how this platform was built up around the pulpit. *(Derek Fellows Collection)*

The Revd W.H. Topliss preaches from the pulpit at the last service held in the Wesley Chapel, Bloxwich, on 7 July 1963. *(Derek Fellows Collection)*

Closing the doors for the last time on 7 July 1963. Left to right: Ray Styche, Derek Fellows, Dr S.G. Phillips (the Trustees' Secretary), the Revd W.H. Topliss, Howard Ford and Norman Boden (chapel stewards). *(Derek Fellows Collection)*

The Primitive Methodists were holding meetings somewhere in Bloxwich by the end of the 1830s. In 1842 they built a basic chapel in the High Street. By the 1890s they had outgrown their first chapel and purchased adjoining ground to build something bigger. The chapel illustrated by the drawing on the right was built in Ruabon brick and was much more imposing. It opened in 1896. By 1902 the original building which had continued in use as a Sunday School was demolished and replaced with new facilities.

The last service at Pinfold Street. The congregation prepare to move to Victoria Road, 27 November 1966. *(Derek Fellows Collection)*

Members of the Methodist New Connexion founded a congregation in Bloxwich in 1854. They opened the chapel seen here, in New Street, in 1894, by which time they were known as the United Methodist Free Church. Like Pinfold Street, the chapel closed on 27 November 1966 in order to amalgamate the Methodist chapels in Bloxwich. *(Church Archives/Derek Fellows)*

St John's Methodist Church, Victoria Street, Bloxwich, 1971. At the beginning of the 1960s the three Methodist congregations in Bloxwich decided to amalgamate and built a brand new church in Victoria Road. It was designed by Hulme, Upright and partners and was built by C. Cornes of Stoke-on-Trent. The building was opened on 3 December 1966. The modern building contrasts with the remains of the 1910 Sunday School building seen on the left. *(Alan Price)*

# 7   West Bromwich

Many chapels in the West Bromwich area were covered in *More Black Country Chapels*, but this time we approach the town from Walsall and Wednesbury and come across some more chapels in the more remote parts of West Bromwich.

Moorlands Methodist Chapel is a good example of a chapel that seems geographically quite close to Wednesbury, but is in fact in West Bromwich. The building seen above was opened in 1959 but it has a history going back much further. The Moorlands congregation began life as a house group on the Moorland Estate in the 1930s. Eventually they found a temporary home in a Scout hut, and then, in about 1940, they amalgamated with the Hall Green Mission and took up residence in the latter's corrugated iron building in Hall Green Road. The Hall Green (Primitive Methodist) Mission had been in existence since 1877, and is seen in the 1951 picture on the right and includes the Manor House in the background. *(Doreen Davies)*

Raising funds to build the Moorlands Chapel was augmented by the sale of Methodist buildings in Witton Lane, Corser Street and Carters Green, and by a £1,000 grant from the Joseph Rank Benevolent Trust. The foundation stone was laid on 18 October 1958 and construction of the £14,000 chapel began. It was designed by Arthur Jesson.

On 27 October 1959 the new chapel in Hall Green Road was opened. Here we see J.B.H. Jones turning the key to the door, watched by the Revd H. Broadbent, the Revd W.O. Phillipson, Arthur Jesson (architect), W.J. Cooper (treasurer), the Revd John Beech and the Revd E. Redvers Jones. The interior is seen below. *(Doreen Davies)*

All the expected auxiliary activities of church and chapel life were soon developed – Guides and Brownies, Boys' Brigade, Sunday School, Men's and Women's groups, pantomimes, etc., but in recent years all these have declined. Here we see the wedding of Mike and Margaret Kennett and Moorlands on 16 March 1968, which was attended by members of the Boys' Brigade at the chapel. Even weddings at modern chapels have declined as couples search for a visually more impressive backdrop to the wedding photos! *(Doreen Davies)*

Back to the good old days in the tin tabernacle in Hall Green Road. The Moorlands Youth Club members pose for a picture at the back of the hall in 1951. *(Doreen Davies)*

Looking towards the front of the wood-panelled interior of the corrugated-iron building in Hall Green Road we see a 1950 Sunday School anniversary in progress. The original congregation of the late 1890s who met in this building were Primitive Methodists but such distinctions no longer applied when the Moorlands congregation began using it before moving to their 1959 building. *(Doreen Davies)*

The Primitive Methodists also built a chapel at Hall End, dating from 1902. This 2006 photograph reveals a larger hall built at the rear of the chapel. This is currently used by the Potters House Fellowship. *(NW)*

The first wedding at Hall End. Geoff Smith married Freda Wilkes on 12 July 1952. The Revd Turner stands in the doorway. *(Freda Smith)*

Freda (on the left of this group) still plays the organ, which was brought to Hall End from the Lyng. The panelling was added in 1966. Left to right: Freda Smith, Anita Lamb, Bill Clifford, Evelyn Farmer, Irene Thompson and the Revd Margaret Eales. *(NW)*

The Hall End Methodist Sunday school lined up in Vicarage Road, West Bromwich, opposite the chapel on an anniversary parade in 1966. Note the chapel itself on the left. *(Irene Thompson)*

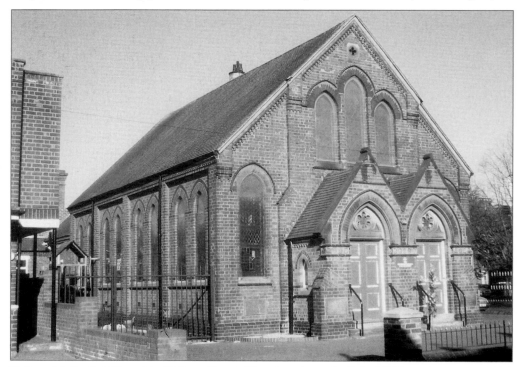

Hallam Methodist Chapel in Hallam Street. The chapel was built in 1883, replacing an 1834 chapel that had existed in Lyndon Street. *(NW)*

The history of Charlemont Methodist Church, seen here in 2006, has been compiled by David Woodman. In the mid-1920s the fields and woods around Charlemont Hall on the outskirts of West Bromwich were about to be engulfed in the spread of new housing. Mr Adam Griffiths of Bustleholme Lane proposed the purchase of a piece of land for a future Methodist chapel. The ground was acquired in June 1926 and the first open-air service was held there on 4 July. Progress was rapid and a temporary wooden building measuring just 30ft × 15ft, was purchased and officially opened on 15 December 1926.

While a host of activities filled the little wooden hut the senior members of the new society planned its brick replacement. The new building was designed by C.E.F. Fillimore and was to be built by F.L. Smith and Sons of Birmingham. The plans included a kitchen, guild room and toilets.

The stone-laying ceremony was held on 21 June 1930. Fifty one-guinea stones were laid on that memorable day. The new building was opened on 25 October 1930 and the first Sunday service was held the following day. The guild room and hut were soon afterwards made available to the West Bromwich Medical Officer of Health for use as maternity and child welfare clinic. Later the hut was used by a Home Guard platoon.

The success of the Sunday School at Charlemont led to continual demands that extra premises be built and made available. Eventually a church hall was opened on 14 May 1960. This was followed by modernisation of the chapel.

In 2003 further modifications were made to the premises at Charlemont. Between these waves of building work, Charlemont has run a host of activities alongside the business of worship and seems to have been a very busy church.

The interior of Charlemont Methodist Church in 2003. The communion rail was a 1954 addition, and during the mid-1960s the pulpit had been moved from a central position. *(David Woodman)*

A Sunday School parade through the Charlemont Farm Estate one sunny day in 1981, led by the band of the Boys' Brigade. The parade is led by Les White, Boys' Brigade leader, and is photographed in Smithmoor Crescent. *(David Woodman Collection)*

The laying of the foundation stone on 21 June 1926 when fifty bricks bought for one guinea each were laid. The girl in white with the mallett is Emily Carter, and the girl in the white cap peering round from the back is Brenda Peckman. *(David Woodman Collection)*

Opening the new hall at Charlemont Methodist Church on 14 May 1960. The hall is being opened by Brenda Peckman, who, as a child, appears in the above photograph. Seen here, left to right: The Revd Redvers Jones, the builder, the Revd John Beech, Geoffrey Cox (architect), -?-, -?-, the Revd Handel Broadbent. *(David Woodman Collection)*

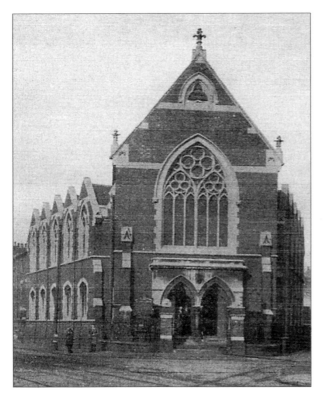

As our survey crosses West Bromwich to look at a chapel in Ryders Green lets look at a couple of other chapels that are now history.

The Wesleyan Methodist Chapel at Carters Green was a well-known local landmark but that did not prevent its demolition in the 1950s when the Methodists were rationalising the number of buildings they used in West Bromwich. It was built on the site of the Junction Inn where roads divided to go to Wednesbury via Hill Top, and Dudley via Great Bridge.

The foundation stone was laid on 4 May 1875 and the chapel opened on 8 May 1876. Galleries and an organ were added in 1888.

Hardware Street United Reform Church replaced the old Congregational chapels in Meeting Street (the 'Ebenezer') and High Street. This photograph was taken on 9 October 2005 and the church closed soon afterwards. Another short-lived suburban church in West Bromwich was Yew Tree Methodist Church, opened on 25 November 1967 and closed in 1995. *(John Hughes)*

Ryders Green Methodist Church occupies a high-profile position at the Greets Green crossroads. The foundation stones were laid in 1873 but the congregation goes back further. A local steel-master, Sir Edward Parkes, was particular interested in this chapel, and had a chapel of his own constructed near his works for the benefit of his employees.

Another stalwart of the chapel was J.T.H. Davies who became the Mayor of West Bromwich. The congregation was augmented with folks from Whitehall Road Chapel when that church closed in 1958. *(NW)*

The interior of Ryders Green Chapel as it is today – the last galleried church in West Bromwich, although the gallery is now little used. The white plasterwork is in stark contrast to the almost black woodwork. *(NW)*

This building at the rear of Ryders Green is doubly important. In the first instance it predates the main chapel, having been built as a Sunday School/chapel in 1856. More recently the building has provided accommodation for a day centre attracting financial support that has helped the church survive. From 1960 to 1967 the chapel was threatened by a compulsory purchase order, but when this was lifted it took on a new lease of life! Help from the Black Country Development Corporation facilitated the creation of the day centre which was opened by Betty Boothroyd MP on 14 April 1984. When this was refurbished Betty came along to reopen it on 23 April 1994. At that time the entrance seen in the above photograph was replaced with a new entrance to the left. (Norman Cooksey)

A Sunday School anniversary picture from Ryders Green, c. 1936. In front of the organ is Alderman Davies, with Mr Whitehouse, the organist, just in front of him. Harold Jones, second from the right, top row, is still alive today to recall the occasion. He married Hilda Spicer who is on the far right of the second row of girls from the top. Sunday School anniversary pictures can be analysed forever in this fashion. (Norman Cooksey)

The first Wesleyan Methodist chapel in Harvills Hawthorn, Hill Top, was built about 1830, but this modern chapel dates only from 1955. The transformation of the 1955 building into the chapel pictured here is told on pages 87 to 89 *(NW)*

Anne Pitt and husband Alan, unveil a window at Hill Top Chapel in memory of her mother, Ivy Round, on 11 June 2006. As explained from page 82 onwards, Ivy Round provides us with a link between three chapels: Greets Green, Great Bridge Street, and Hill Top. *(NW)*

The Revd Frank Cooke and the choir at Hill Top Methodist Chapel on 11 June 2006, the occasion of the dedication of the Ivy Round Memorial window. *(NW)*

Ivy Round provides a link between three chapels: Greets Green, Great Bridge Street, and Hill Top. She is seen here with the Revd Howard Reece at Great Bridge Street. Ivy was born on 27 May 1915, the daughter of a Methodist lay preacher. She grew up as part of the congregation at Greets Green Primitive Methodist Chapel and by her early teens was playing the organ at the Christian Endeavour Meetings, and piano at the Sunday School. She later became youth club leader, choirmistress and church organist.

At the age of eighteen she began writing and producing the concert parties and pantomimes which her father christened 'The Evergreens'.

When the Greets Green chapel closed in 1958 Ivy and family transferred to Great Bridge Street, Great Bridge and then, in 2002 to Hill Top.

Ivy died on 19 May 2005, and was organist at Hill Top right up to the time of her death. *(Ivy Round Archive via Anne Pitt)*

The Greets Green Primitive
Methodist Chapel in Whitehall
Road, West Bromwich. The
congregation traced its history
back its beginnings in 1848 –
a year after the Primitive
Methodists had completed the
Queen Street chapel as the
centre of their operations in
West Bromwich, and a time
when they were building small
chapels in a number of the
villages which eventually
formed West Bromwich. It
appears to have been rebuilt
by the time this picture was
taken in 1948 while the
chapel was celebrating its
centenary. It closed ten years
later. The narrow entry on the
left led through to the Sunday
School and youth club
buildings. *(Anne Pitt)*

The Evergreens present *Babes in the Wood* as their 1945 pantomime at Greets Green
Methodist Chapel. It was written and produced by Ivy Round who is seen standing second
from the right in the back row. Ivy later became a steward and church secretary, and
maintained her work for the Christian Endeavour, the Junior Missionary Association and a
travel group who called themselves 'The Globetrotters'. *(Anne Pitt)*

Ivy Round also organised the Greets Green Methodist Church Sunday School's float in the annual carnival, seen here being overtaken by a West Bromwich Corporation bus in the late 1940s. In fact, Ivy created the annual Greets Green Carnival itself, and it was held on the first Saturday in October. In 1983, at the age of sixty-seven, Ivy attended a Buckingham Palace garden party in recognition of all her community work. *(Anne Pitt)*

When the Greets Green Chapel in Whitehall Road closed Ivy Round (and the Evergreens) had to find a new home at the Great Bridge Street Methodist Church. Ivy is seen here at Great Bridge Street on 25 September 1988 with the Revd Frank Cooke and the Revd Barbara Halstead, on the occasion of Ivy's daughter's wedding. This chapel, built in 1882–3, was also once home to the Primitive Methodists. It closed in August 2002, and the building has now become a snooker hall. *(Anne Pitt)*

The austere interior of Great Bridge Street Chapel was enhanced by the cast-iron columns in this early picture featuring the reversible benches, harmonium and piano. Later a pipe organ was installed but the bare brickwork survived until the end. *(Anne Pitt)*

The Men's Service at Great Bridge Street, West Bromwich, April 1997. It was organised by Joseph Howes who can be seen far left on the back row. The preacher on that occasion was Bill Clifford, seen far left on the front row. *(Anne Pitt)*

The Evergreens continue their work at Great Bridge Street. Anne Pitt (née Round) appears in the centre of this mid-1960s *Babes in the Wood* line-up, and Ivy Round appears on the extreme right.

The Nativity Play at Great Bridge Street was photographed on 17 December 1967. Harold Yates, Sunday School superintendent, is behind the pulpit with Ivy Round on his left. Fifth from the right in the front row is Joan Howes (née Smith), playing Maid Marion, having graduated from her first role as a robin, seen on the front row on page 83! *(Anne Pitt)*

The Young People's section of the choir at an early 1990s children's festival anniversary at Great Bridge Street Methodist Church, the Sunday School having closed by then. Anne Pitt sits behind her mother, Ivy Round, on the left of the second and third rows. *(Anne Pitt)*

A Wesleyan Methodist chapel had existed in Harvills Hawthorn, Hill Top, since 1830. It declined in the 1940s and in 1955 this building was erected in New Street to replace it, although at first it was simply intended to be used as a Sunday School. Two major refurbishments have created something more striking, and in 2002 the congregation was swelled by the addition of folks from Great Bridge Street. *(Mary Reynolds)*

The 1955 building at Hill Top was made suitable as a place of worship, making discreet use of the stage but still looking like a rather stark church hall. *(Mary Reynolds)*

The old heaters and light fittings remain but after the first refurbishment at Hill Top the stage was curtained off and a panelled area was created with fittings that came from Birmingham Central Hall, and which conveniently fitted the proscenium arch. Norman Reynolds, the organist, is on the right of the back row, and the Revd Barbara Halstead is in the centre. *(Olive Ellis)*

At the end of the 1990s the Methodist Chapel at Hill Top underwent another major refurbishment. A new wooden font, made from an old communion rail, was made by John Chambers, seen here in his workshop. *(Olive Ellis)*

Stained-glass windows from the original chapel in Harvills Hawthorn were rebuilt by John Hardman, watched in this picture by the Revd Keith Pearce. The windows, now installed in the chapel, had been 'lost' in store for many years. The old flat roof was replaced and a new entrance was created. *(Olive Ellis)*

Cllr George Turton and Mrs Price, the oldest member of the congregation, open the new entrance doors to the refurbished Hill Top Methodist Church on 22 May 1999.

A Primitive Methodist Chapel was built at Golds Green, Harvills Hawthorn, in about 1836. It was rebuilt in this form in 1912, and closed in 1969. It has since been acquired and refurbished by the Triumphant Church of God, as seen here in this 2006 photograph. (NW)

# 8    Both Sides of the Stour

The River Stour rises in the Clent Hills and runs through Halesowen before turning westwards towards Stourbridge. As it passes between Cradley and Quarry Bank it forms the former boundary between Worcestershire and Staffordshire in an area that is really the southernmost part of the Black Country. Beyond Stourbridge it passes through Wollaston before leaving the south-western frontier of the Black Country.

At the point where the Stour is joined by the Mousesweet Brook, at Cradley Forge, the early Dissenters built the first non-conformist chapel in the Black Country. This was the southern boundary of the old Pensnett Chase and therefore the building was known as Pensnett Chapel, first registered in 1704. It was burnt down in 1715 and had to be rebuilt. In 1796 the congregation left the building, crossed the Stour and began again at Park Lane, Netherend (see page 110 of *Black Country Chapels*).

In this chapter we begin our survey in Cradley, proceed to Quarry Bank and then call briefly at Wollaston.

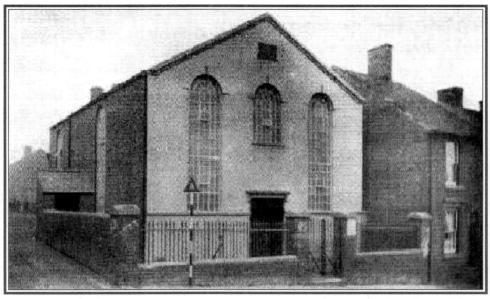

The chapels of Cradley are described in *Black Country Chapels* on pages 109 to 112 but by no means comprehensively. We return to Cradley to look at the history of Providence Chapel, Windmill Hill – a chapel which celebrated it 150th anniversary in 2006. 1856 was the year in which the land was sold to the chapel's founding trustees. The chapel seen above opened on 5 April 1857, and aligned itself with the Methodist New Connexion.

Sunday School provision was always very important at Providence and in 1868 a small Sunday School building was erected behind the chapel. In 1886 it was replaced with a bigger building and in 1925 construction of a third building culminated in its opening on 10 December. Two years later the old chapel had to be abandoned and worship moved into the 1886 Sunday School building. The building still exists today. *(Derek Trickett)*

In June 1963 the congregation at Providence were able to move into this building. It is interesting to note that Joseph Tate built the 1886 building and that his company, J.M. Tate, built both the 1925 and 1963 buildings. The 1925 building has now become the church hall. On 30 July 2006 balloons were released in front of the 1963 chapel to celebrate the 150th anniversary. *(John James )*

## Quarry Bank

We have already referred to the early eighteenth-century chapel, or meeting house, built by Dissenters at Cradley Forge – an area we would now regard as part of Quarry Bank. Even a century later, in the early nineteenth century, Quarry Bank was still a collection of scattered hamlets inhabited by colliers, chain-makers and nailers. The creation of a new parish and the building of Christ Church in the mid-1840s is testimony to the fact that the village was growing and the hamlets were being loosely joined into a single community. Meanwhile the Methodists were at work establishing chapels in these hamlets. Eventually the village enjoyed the use of two Primitive Methodist chapels, two New Connexion chapels, a Wesleyan Chapel, a Congregational Chapel and eventually a little Pentecostal church. The latter is described on pages 145 and 146).

It is not clear what happened to the old building after the congregation at the old Pensnett Chapel left the Stour valley at Cradley Forge in 1796 to re-establish themselves at Park Lane. In 1850 a new chapel was built near this spot, but closer to the foot of Hammer Bank. It was built by Methodists of the New Connexion, and although it lasted until 1938 no photograph of it has been found. Even its exact location is now obscured by the realignment of the road. Ten years earlier the congregation had started building a new Sunday School building at the top of Hammer Bank, which opened on 7 July 1928 (see page 4 of *Black Country Chapels*). It was designed by Messrs Gething and Rolley who later designed Quarry Bank's Congregational Chapel.

In 1938 the Sunday School building became the church itself, although it still had to be dual-purpose and was home to the famous local amateur dramatic society. Proceeds from their shows paid off the mortgage on the building.

In this 1998 photograph we see a path descending Hammer Bank down to the River Stour and the chapel resting beyond in its rather secluded position. *(NW)*

Some of the folks at Cradley Forge Methodist Church pose for a photograph at a musical evening on 8 September 2002. In the pulpit are the late Sybil Genner, who had presided over the event, and Brian Clarke, Sunday School superintendent. *(NW)*

By the 1820s Primitive Methodist missionaries were also active among the working communities of Quarry Bank, particularly lower Quarry Bank, close to the Stour. In the 1830s they probably used an old nail warehouse close to Sheffield Street – a building which eventually became Christ Church's church hall. In 1845 they seem to have built a chapel in Rose Hill but had outgrown that by 1860. They were then able to move into a new chapel in New Street. The land on the chapel's side of New Street tended to slip down towards the Stour. The 1860 chapel finally gave way to subsidence in 1897. The Prims were not deterred and built the chapel seen in this picture on the same site. It opened in 1903 and survived until 1981.

The Primitive Methodists in New Street seem to have wanted to spread their influence to remoter parts of Quarry Bank and in 1884 they built a small wooden chapel or mission in Birch Coppice. Four years later the original building was moved for further use at the Hayes and was replaced with a brand new tin tabernacle. It is seen here in 1958 while awaiting demolition following the opening of its brick successor. *(Joy Woodhouse)*

The brick chapel at Birch Coppice opened in August 1958. Here we see the congregation gathering outside the chapel after the anniversary service on 5 May 2002. *(NW)*

The Wesleyan Methodists built an early chapel at the other end of Quarry Bank in Mount Pleasant. This opened in 1828, seventeen years before the Anglicans built the parish church in Quarry Bank. It was probably built to serve a wide area, some of which was still very rural. The original frontage of the building was obscured by a new porch-like extension in 1927, sponsored by Ernest Stevens, a well known local benefactor whose wife had grown up in the congregation. In 1839 and again in 1907 the chapel folk had been forced to purchase coal seams below the chapel to safeguard its existence.

The bottom photograph on the opposite page was taken in about 1930, and the above picture show changes in the interior of the Mount Pleasant Chapel. The above picture was taken just after a refurbishment that took place in the summer of 1978. Since then the pews have been removed. The large stained-glass window, which has been retained as a key feature of the chapel, was also provided by Ernest Stevens during the 1927 modernisation of the building. Until the 1927 rebuild, the interior had been very plain and the chapel had also contained a three-sided gallery. *(Chapel Collection/Olive Allchurch)*

One can be excused for thinking this is another chapel interior, but it is in fact the interior of the detached Sunday School building built at the back of the Mount Pleasant chapel. This building, replacing earlier ones, was built in 1902, and opened on 27 October of that year. *(Chapel Collection)*

In the absence of any present-day Sunday School scholars, the Wesleyan Methodist Chapel at Mount Pleasant now holds an annual Sunday School reunion. This picture was taken in May 2002. During the 2007 event Emma Hanglin (front row, third from left) and Olive Allchurch (sixth from left) were boasting that they were the only two present who could claim to have been attending the chapel for over eighty years. *(NW)*

The Ganner brothers were among six members of the Ganner family to found at the Wesley Chapel Mount Pleasant on 13 May 2007 for the annual reunion service. Alan Ganner sits at the organ console, having been a professional organist at one time. Mick Ganner, who was preaching on 13 May 2007, had at one time been pastor of the Congregational Chapel in Quarry Bank High Street. *(NW)*

Although this is a poor photograph it is the only one to have come to light showing the former New Connexion Methodist chapel that once stood in Mount Pleasant, Quarry Bank. It was taken in August 1925 just after the reopening of the chapel, by then known as the United Methodists.

In 1836 eight of the eleven trustees of the Wesleyan Chapel in Mount Pleasant resigned and broke away from the Wesleyan branch of Methodism. It seems that they allied themselves with the New Connexion and, at some stage, erected a chapel on the opposite side of the road about 200 yards away. It is listed in a New Connexion circuit plan of 1838. Unfortunately the site was also much afflicted by subsidence and the chapel had to be abandoned in 1907. The congregation then met in the Sunday School building while trying to collect funds to rebuild the chapel. It was reopened in the form seen above on 12 August 1925 by Mrs Cartwright – then the oldest member of the congregation. The key she used is illustrated in *More Black Country Chapels*, page 143.

The Congregationalists in Quarry Bank have an equally obscure history. During the 1870s an independent faction began meeting in an ex-industrial building near Merry Hill called 'The Soap Hole'. One suggestion is that congregation grew out of the Blue Ribbon Army movement – a temperance organisation that made some progress in the Black Country in the 1870s. In later years the congregation stated that it had come into existence in 1874. By 1897 they had affiliated with the Congregational Union and had moved into Z Street, just off Quarry Bank High Street. In 1935 the Z Street building was relegated to Sunday School duties when the Congregational Church on the High Street was opened.

The Z Street building is seen here in 1966 just before it was replaced by a new Sunday School building facing the High Street. At some stage Z Street was renamed Chapel Street. *(Alan Southall)*

The Congregational Church (replacing the Z Street Chapel) was opened on 6 July 1935. It was built by A.J. Crump of Dudley and was designed by Messrs Gething and Rolley. The Sunday School building next door was added in 1967. *(NW)*

A Sunday School anniversary scene at the Congregational Chapel in Quarry Bank on 19 May 2002. The adults include teachers Hannah Warwick, Angela Hodgetts and Ruth Stuart, the superintendent, Vera Wright and church secretary, Ian Smith. *(NW)*

## Wollaston

The Stour heads westwards from Stourbridge passing the village of Wollaston on its way. The parish church, St James's, was opened in 1859 as a result of carving a new parish out of the area once covered by the parish of Oldswinford. A Methodist chapel was built in Bright Street in 1891. This was replaced in 1960–1 with a modern building facing Cobden Street. The Brethren opened a corrugated-iron Gospel Hall on the corner of Eggington Road in 1926 and this is now known as the Wollaston Evangelical Church. (See page 28 of *Black Country Chapels*).

The most interesting non-conformist church in Wollaston is the Wollaston Free Church, seen above in May 2007 while celebrating its fortieth anniversary. The congregation was formed by a group of Baptists from South Street, Stourbridge, led by the Revd Peter Williams. They took over the former Stourbridge Rugby Club building, in Somerset Drive, Wollaston, in February 1967 and the first service was held on 13 May 1967. The building occupying this site has undergone several major transformations over the years, including the acquisition of a spire during the 1970s. A new foyer and entrance was added in 1985 and then major rebuilding took place in 2000 when a new roof was put on making the worship area very lofty and visually impressive. In time for the church's fortieth anniversary in May 2007 considerable work was completed on two lounge spaces, a new lift and improved access.

Peter Williams and the rugby club in 1967. (*Express & Star*)

Wollaston Free Church. The effect of raising the ceiling during the 2000 rebuild is well illustrated in this 2007 picture. The church has been through fifteen alterations in its forty-year life, and the fellowship now can be proud of the appearance of its church and its facilities. Although the name Free Church suggests the kind of independence seen in many other Black Country churches, this church is in effect a Baptist church. *(NW)*

The choir at Wollaston Free Church taking its part in the fortieth anniversary service, 13 May 2007, after a fortnight of celebrations and anniversary activities. These had included a children's service, an evening of reminiscence and an evening of home-produced variety entertainment. *(NW)*

# 9    Gospel Halls

Across the Black Country, and all over the world, are non-conformists who reject the idea of being a denomination like the Methodists, Baptists, etc. They also usually reject the need for central organisation and an ordained ministry, preferring local independence and a lay leadership. They prefer the word assembly to church or chapel, and the function of the premises in which they meet is to provide a base in which to pursue the proclamation of the Gospel – hence the term gospel hall.

The movement began in the early nineteenth century and its followers are often called Brethren, but it must be remembered that it is outsiders who might like to invent such a label, rather than the people themselves. What they have in common is an evangelical stance that links them to missionary work, to crusades and tent missions, to giving out tracts and the simplicity of open-air services. The assemblies themselves often remain small, and if they grow large they often divide. Families are the bedrock of Brethren assemblies with great continuity from generation to generation and a researcher soon encounters the same names reappearing in the stories of each assembly.

They tend to steer clear of ecumenical trends in modern Christianity, and their other-worldliness seems to have made them fairly uninterested in their own history. All this makes it quite difficult to detail their institutions in a book such as this. Compared with the world of Methodism, etc., they leave little historical information for the rest of us to pick up.

Many assemblies grew out of the work of a particular crusade or mission, in the same way that Pentecostal assemblies grew out of the Jeffreys brothers' mission of 1930, which will be dealt with in a subsequent chapter. In this chapter we look at some of the Black Country assemblies that grew up from the late nineteenth and early twentieth century onwards, and future historians will have to try to sort out the many modern evangelical movements that have been created in more recent times.

This is a story that includes the Hebron Hall, Horseley Heath; the Bethesda Hall, Holloway Bank/Hill Top; the Hellier Street Gospel Hall in Dudley; the West Bromwich Street Gospel Hall, Oldbury; the Hargate Lane Hall in West Bromwich; the Wellcroft Street and Price Road Halls in Wednesbury; the Caldmore Evangelistic Mission in Walsall; the Rough Hay Gospel Hall in Darlaston; the Hasbury Gospel Hall near Halesowen and the Westbury Chapel in Wolverhampton. The hall in Wollaston was mentioned on page 28 of *Black Country Chapels*.

The Hebron Hall, Horseley Heath. Three brothers, Albert, George and Henry Hughes of Tipton worshipped at the Lea Brook Primitive Methodist Chapel until about 1892 when they left and joined the Wellcroft Street Gospel Hall in Wednesbury. They decided to plant a chapel nearer home and in 1902 formed an assembly that met in a rented room in the Miners' Hall, Great Bridge.

They established a Sunday School, and by about 1919 were able to invite a Yorkshire evangelist named Philip Mills to meetings held at the new Palace Cinema on the corner of Slater Street, Great Bridge. As the assembly grew they began to think about acquiring their own premises.

Land was bought at Horseley Heath and an ex-Army hut of corrugated-iron construction was purchased in the aftermath of the First World War. It had been a reading room and was found at Newhaven, Sussex. Benjamin Hall went down to Newhaven and arranged for it to be dismantled and sent back to Tipton by rail.

This was erected on substantial brick footings and opened in October 1921. It was opened with a grand march of the congregation from Great Bridge to their new hall. Although the iron cladding has been removed and the sides are now brick, the arrangement of the windows and buttresses reminds one of the building's origins even today. The floor was put in at a height sufficient to provide space for a baptismal pool, and the front of the building was made from brick. Since then the side walls have been bricked and a rear extension has been developed. In recent times a new side entrance and ramp have been added. From simply calling itself the Hebron Hall, it now uses the name Hebron Gospel Hall.

From 1921 until the mid-1950s the Hebron enjoyed strong membership of about 100 people, plus a Sunday School of anything up to 150 children, led by Arthur Simkins. The assembly's annual red-letter day was not an anniversary, but the Annual Bible Teaching Conference. For years the assembly also continued the tradition of open-air worship and regularly made their way down to the Market Place in Great Bridge to preach there after Sunday evening service.

A gospel choir from Birmingham filled the platform at the Hebron Hall, Horseley Heath, on Sunday evening in the summer of 2006. *(NW)*

Bethesda, Witton Lane, Hill Top. The modern Bethesda Chapel standing in Witton Lane today has an interesting history, carefully put on the record by the late Charles Walter Phillips (1909–2004), one of the trustees.

The congregation was established by the efforts of Joseph Hewitt, a boot and shoe maker and repairer. In 1891 he came to Hill Top, having previously worked in Walsall and Wednesbury. He organised cottage meetings and tent services, helped by visiting evangelists.

In 1893 land in Holloway Bank was leased from the Patent Shaft and Axletree Company and a tin tabernacle building was erected. In other words the congregation prepared the site and dug the foundations and then assembled their chapel by erecting a timber frame and cladding the exterior with sheets of corrugated-iron. They called themselves the Hill Top Christian Mission. *(Gillian Snaith)*

The Iron Mission Room, which had cost £112, was opened on 22 May 1893, and regular services commenced six days later. At the beginning the assembly consisted of just six members. Their membership grew and the building was enlarged in 1922 under the direction of Benjamin Hall of the Oldbury Assembly. It was at this time that the name Bethesda was adopted.

The period of expansion came in 1947 when the assembly tried to obtain extra land from West Bromwich Corporation. It was originally hoped, during the 1950s, that it would be possible to build around the existing and deteriorating iron building. In the end the assembly was allocated a new site on land in Witton Lane.

Plans for the present building were prepared by Mr Bissell and handed over to the architect, Mr C.E. Davies of Walsall. It was built by H. Tomlinson and Son for just over £7,500 and then had to be furnished – quite a contrast to the original chapel's construction costs! The new Bethesda was opened on the evening of Saturday 22 July 1961.

More recently the assembly at Bethesda has been joined by Brethren from Hargate Lane, West Bromwich.

*Above:* The Bethesda, Witton Lane, 2006. *(NW)*
*Left:* A Christmas party in the old tin mission on Holloway Bank, *c.* 1950. Back row, left to right: Bill Perry, Walter Phillips, Joseph Massey, Sid Lane, Michael Harper, -?-, Jack Grice, Mary Coleman, Rhoda Lees, Doris Phillips, Lilian Phillips, Florrie Shires. Front row: Rose Berry, Vera Potter, Elsie Steen, Joan Croton, Thelma Walker. *(Gillian Snaith)*

The Wellcroft Street Gospel Hall in Wednesbury appears to have begun life as a Quaker Meeting House but in 1914 it was sold by F.H. Lloyd to the Brethren, who may have previously rented it for some time as they claimed to be the first Brethren Fellowship in the area. In 1924 they greatly enlarged the premises by building the hall seen on the right in the above picture. The date 1924 appears on the building. Ironically it was the deteriorating condition of the newer hall that led to the whole site being sold for demolition. The remaining fourteen members of the assembly moved in May 2003 to join the folks at Price Road. In 2007 the building in Wellcroft Street still stands, all boarded up, and its Gospel Hall sign is disappearing behind undergrowth.

The picture above dates from the early 1930s and shows the Sunday School pupils at Wellcroft Street gathering outside the building before marching off to the railway station for the annual treat.

The Wellcroft Street Assembly supported missions to Rough Hay and to Price Road, resulting in gospel halls being built in both places. *(Ray Walker)*

In 1954 a team from Wellcroft Street set up a Sunday School in Walton Road Junior School in Price Road. Prayer meetings grew from this and ultimately the folks at Price Road became an autonomous fellowship. In 2003 they were joined by brothers and sisters from Wellcroft Street when that assembly had to close. *(NW)*

On page 7 of *More Black Country Chapels* I included a picture of the interior of the Oldbury Gospel Hall, taken in 1983, as the hall was being demolished. Now it is possible to feature a picture of the exterior of the building and add something of its history.

Benjamin Hall, who was once part of the assembly at Hebron, Horseley Heath, felt the need to establish a fellowship in Oldbury and they first met at Knight's Engineering Works in Market Street. This building was erected in West Bromwich Street, adjacent to the canal, in about 1932. The main hall and baptistry was upstairs, and the Sunday School met below. *(Don Sheldon via John Evans)*

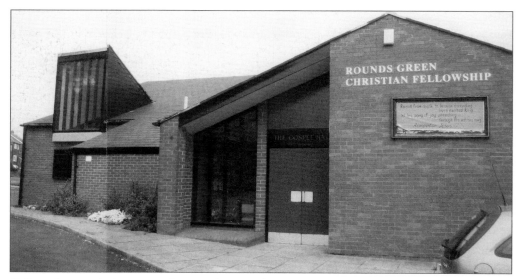

Oldbury's population moved towards Round Green as the town declined and awaited redevelopment. The chapels moved as well. As the Gospel Hall closed in West Bromwich Street in April 1983, the fellowship itself moved to new premises in St James Road, Rounds Green. Although they use the modern term Christian Fellowship, the words Gospel Hall still appear above the door. *(NW)*

The Hellier Street Gospel Hall at Hellier Street, Dudley, now seems to be sinking below the road, as seen in this 2006 photograph. The key person who played a part in developing this assembly was Evan Griffiths, a herbalist and chemist of King Street. In the 1920s he formed an assembly that met in a room above the post office in Salop Street, Eve Hill, but this was a long way from the Flood Street area where he felt a mission would be of greater use. Eventually he found this plot of land in Hellier Street and the members of the assembly raised money and built the hall themselves. Although the sign on the building suggests that it opened in 1931, it seems likely that it opened before Evan Griffiths' death in December 1930.

A Hellier Street Gospel Hall summer outing to Church Stretton, 1950s. On the right of the group stands Bill Horan who was caretaker of the hall for many years. His wife, Elsie, is sixth from the right and she kept the hall clean. Elsie, who is still alive at the time of writing was a member of the assembly before they moved to Hellier Street and was there when the new hall opened. (*Eunice Eaves Collection*)

Elsie Horan presides with teapot in hand at Hellier Street Gospel Hall ladies' sewing class in the late 1950s. She stands in a platform-mounted pulpit, built by Benjamin Hall of Oldbury and Hebron, all of which has been removed. Back row, left to right: Hilda Smart, Gladys Darby, Florrie Lloyd, Esther Darby, Maureen Boardman. Front row: Mary Bullock, Margaret Darby and Jean Smart. *(Eunice Eaves Collection)*

The front of the Hellier Street Gospel Hall has also changed over the years. Compare the picture on page 109 with this picture taken on 9 March 1957 at the wedding of Sheila Ashman and John Smart. Left to right: Hazel Brooks, Maureen Yates, Valentine Shaw, John Smart, Sheila Smart, Gillian Dudley and Matthew Ashman. *(John and Sheila Smart)*

The Sunday School at Hellier Street was an immediate success, and even after the slum clearance schemes in the Flood Street area, a recent generation of Asian children from the streets adjoining Hellier Street kept the numbers high for a while. This group, photographed in about 1950, is probably the Saturday Afternoon Group, rather than the Sunday School. The adults in the second and third rows are as follows (men): Jack Marsh, Gerald Mills, Walter Massey, James Smart, Bill Horan, Ken Evans; (ladies): Hazel Trumper, Mary Hill, May Middleton, Eunice Horan, Margaret Rayden and Mary Bullock.

    The bare brick walls seen in this picture have since been plastered, and the curtain across the hall to create a vestry has disappeared as the hall has been extended and improved. The old benches have long since been replaced. *(Eunice Eaves Collection)*

The author, Ned Williams, addresses Black Country Society members on a visit to the Hellier Street Gospel Hall in May 2006. *(Graham Beckley)*

## Gospel Halls and the Brethren in Walsall

A Brethren assembly was established in Walsall in the 1860s in Bridge Street and later moved to Burrowes Street, but had closed altogether by the 1960s.

In about 1914 a group of young people who were part of the Baptist congregation at Vicarage Walk Chapel decided to break away. At first they rented a room in a public house at Caldmore Green for their Sunday morning service, but soon were involved in trying to find their own premises.

They found land and a semi-derelict workshop building at the back of some houses in West Bromwich Street. Using their own skills and talents they renovated this building and opened it on 18 November 1918 as the Caldmore Mission. About the same time Mr William Field moved into the area from Sutton where he had been a member of the Brethren. He provided leadership for this young congregation, and once affiliated to the Brethren, they became known as the Caldmore Gospel Hall. The Gospel Hall in its early form is illustrated above.

In about 1920 a successful Sunday School was inaugurated and the Gospel Hall flourished. The assembly still meets in the same building today but it has undergone many improvements, including the inclusion of a baptistry. William Field left in the early 1930s and others have led since, but the Gospel Hall has witnessed great changes, both to the building, its surroundings and the congregation. There is no longer a Sunday School, the congregation has dispersed and is no longer dominated by people living close by. The houses in West Bromwich Street have gone and access to a car park is now from Little London. The little Gospel Hall, seen below in a recent picture, is now dwarfed by its new neighbour, a Sikh temple.

A Brethren Hall was built in the Delves in 1931 in Talke Road. The original wooden building was replaced by the brick building seen here in 1958. It has since closed but is now used by another fellowship. The missionary spirit also inspired the building of Stephenson Hall on the Beechdale Estate in 1957. The latter was built by Frank Bissell who had been brought up as a member of the Wellcroft Street Assembly in Wednesbury and had later joined the Brethren at Burrowes Street, Walsall. He built Stephenson Hall as a new home for fellow Brethren from Burrowes Street, and for the community on the Beechdale Estate. It opened on 7 June 1958, but failed in both respects and in 1964 it became the home of the Bethel Temple assembly from Queen Street (see page 62).

The Hargate Lane Gospel Hall, West Bromwich, was built in about 1934 by a group of West Bromwich Christians who felt the need to provide an assembly meeting place in this part of the town. The last service was held here in February 2005 and the members of the assembly moved to join those at Bethesda, Witton Lane. Two members of the assembly continue to run community youth and childcare services from the building. (NW)

The little Gospel Hall in Hall Street, Willenhall, was originally an industrial building belonging to William Tildesley Ltd, and was hidden from Hall Street by houses. The fellowship was formed by young people from the Little London Baptists, who had been saved and wanted to start afresh. First calling itself the Hall Street Mission, it was founded on 8 May 1941 and the first service was held three days later under blackout conditions! Although remaining a small fellowship, the Sunday School prospered until children disappeared from the area as a result of slum clearance. *(NW)*

A wartime Sunday School anniversary in the Hall Street Mission, Willenhall. Note the bare walls of the building's interior, the blackout blinds and the gas-lit chandelier. *(Bernard Appleby)*

By way of contrast, here is the fellowship in their cosy wood-lined interior, November 2006. Back row: Bernard Appleby (one of the founders), Stuart Smith, Tony and Kath Sankey, Esme Till. Middle row: Stan Partridge, Maurice Proffitt, Joan Riley, Bill Till, Brian Bennett. Front row: Grace Partridge, Martha Hathersmith, Alice ?, Frank Lonney (visiting preacher), and Ryan ?. *(Tony Sankey)*

The wooden shed in Peacock Road, Darlaston, out of which grew the Rough Hay Gospel Hall (as described on the next page). *(Reg Bennett Collection)*

Following a tented crusade in Darlaston at the end of the 1930s, Alfred Hardy Lycett of Wednesbury Road, Walsall, began his gospel work in the Rough Hay Estate, then only partly built.

During the summer of 1939 the elderly Mr Lycett worked continuously at Rough Hay telling everyone that ARP stood for 'A Real Pardon' for those who would be saved. Thursday evening meetings began in Mrs Bliss's home in Rough Hay Road and then, in August 1939, Mr Lycett bought a wooden canteen building from Moxley Brickworks and erected it on the corner of Peacock Road.

The 20ft × 14ft shed was ready to receive its first Sunday School scholars on 3 September 1939 – the day the Second World War began. The shed was extended at least once but the congregation longed for the day when it could be replaced by a brick building.

The picture below shows the brick Gospel Hall, facing Hall Street East, nearing completion in 1953. The old wooden hut can still be seen next door, but is facing Peacock Road. As can be seen in the picture above, a brick wall and fence was completed by the time the hall opened on Saturday 14 November 1953. One member of the fellowship at Rough Hay was Reg Bennett who later became well known as a guide at the Black Country Museum. Before he died, Reg collected together an archive of material relating to the history of the Gospel Hall, and began writing its history. *(Reg Bennett Collection)*

The pulpit and organ in the original wooden hut at Rough Hay with a ghostly image of Reg Bennett on the rostrum in about 1943. The organ was donated by Mrs Homer but no-one could play it so it was often used to separate adjacent Sunday School classes.

The rostrum in the new brick-built Rough Hay Gospel Hall, 1953. The rostrum survives today but the panelling at the back has now been removed. Left to right: Albert Stanley, Frank Bissell, the builder, unidentified visiting speaker and Harold Homer. Frank Bissell built several gospel halls including the one at Beechdale (see page 62). *(Reg Bennett Collection)*

The Gospel Hall in Albert Road, Hasbury, on the outskirts of Halesowen, was built by an assembly that first met above the Co-op in Peckingham Street on 24 June 1934. The hall, seen here in a 2007 photograph, was opened on 13 May 1939. The church was renamed Hasbury Christian Fellowship in 1978, and new community facilities were added in 1987. Worship still takes place in the old hall, on the left, but there are plans to replace this with something more modern. *(NW)*

One event that has brought the Gospel Halls of the Black Country together has been the annual Missionary Conference. Here we see the 1954 conference platform at Wellcroft Street. The picture includes Brethren from local halls plus missionaries and their wives. Here we catch a glimpse of Frank Bissell (second from right, middle row), Geoffrey Bull whose work in Tibet became famous (second from right, back row) and the Becketts from the Hellier Street hall who missioned in Pakistan. *(Ray Walker)*

In Wolverhampton the Brethren first met in Clarence Street in 1885, later moving to an old chapel in Cleveland Street. In 1962 they moved into the new Westbury Chapel just off Broad Street, the present home of the annual Missionary Conference. In December 2006 members of the Ladies Group and friends are seen celebrating the centenary of their Monday afternoon fellowship at the Westbury Chapel, Wolverhampton. (See pages 131 and 132 of *More Black Country Chapels*). *(Express & Star)*

# 10    The Elim Churches

George Jeffreys (1889–1962) came from a Congregational background in South Wales. At the age of fifteen, he was saved and converted during the Welsh Revival of 1904. Between 1915 and 1934 he was a very active Pentecostal revivalist and his crusades brought him to the Black Country. He created the Elim Evangelistic Band in 1915 but by 1934 this had become the Elim Foursquare Gospel Alliance. The name Elim comes from the book of *Exodus* and refers to an oasis to which the Israelites were led by Moses. The foursquare element is the vision of Christ in four roles: Saviour, Healer, Baptiser and Coming King.

George Jeffreys withdrew from the Elim Church in 1939 and formed the Bible-Pattern Fellowship, and at least one Black Country fellowship took the same path. One of George Jeffreys' most successful crusades had been in Birmingham but in the Black Country his influence seems to have been more modest. Currently there seem to be five Elim churches in the Black Country: at Dudhill Road, Rowley Regis; at Beamore Road, Old Hill; at Crankhall Lane, Friar Park, Wednesbury and Victoria Street, West Bromwich, and at Cardale Street, Blackheath, where the Elim and Assembly of God fellowships have worked together as the Flame Church. The Zion Christian Centre in Halesowen is also aligned with the Elim Pentecostal Church.

The little Elim Church in Beamore Road, Old Hill, carries a stone indicating that it was built in 1955, although the railings are a recent addition. Like many Black Country chapels, this one is off the beaten track. *(NW)*

The Elim Church, Dudley, first met in 1933 in an upper room above the Dartmouth Garage in the outer reaches of Dudley High Street. In 1956 a new minister, the Revd Baxter, managed to obtain the use of the old church hall of Christ Church Congregational Chapel on the corner of North Street (see page 76 of *More Black Country Chapels*). Above we see Pastor Jones leading a late 1950s Sunday School parade though Kates Hill, an area then well served by the Elim Church in North Street. *(Bill Webb Collection)*

Pastor Dyke, District Superintendent of the Elim Churches, turns the key to open the door in the ex-church hall in North Street in May 1956. Pastor Baxter looks on. *(Bill Webb Collection)*

## Elim in West Bromwich

In 1936 two Elim evangelists, the Barrie brothers, were invited to West Bromwich to conduct a crusade. A fledgling church, led by Pastor Ward, grew out of their work and began to hold services in a corrugated-iron hut at Carters Green. The hut had been known as the Labour Church, a secular church created by the Independent Labour Party. This was one of at least two such institutions created in the Black Country, the other being at King Street, Dudley.

The Elim fellowship moved from the hut in about 1938 to the upper floor of the Ruskin Hall on the corner of Lombard Street. The room at the Ruskin Hall was cold and inconvenient and the fellowship temporarily moved back to the Labour Church in 1939. At the end of the war the Elim Church attempted to rent a building belonging to the Catholic Apostolic Church in Victoria Street. The building had been badly bomb-damaged and was no longer in use. The Catholic Apostolic Church was as unusual an organisation as the Labour Church and had its origins in America. Only a handful of such churches existed in Britain, practising a mixture of Catholicism and fervent Adventism. The local representative, or Angel, was a Mr Thonga in Birmingham. He eventually allowed the Elim folk to move in.

In 1972 the Elim Fellowship completed the purchase of the former Catholic Apostolic Church and also completed its modernisation and refurbishment. The old Victorian building has been demolished and a new purpose-built community church has now been provided.

The interior of the hut used by the Elim assembly in West Bromwich from 1936 to 1938 and briefly again in 1939. Erected to provide a home for meetings of a secular or humanistic style, it is interesting to consider that it became home to a modern Christian movement. *(Kevin Turner Collection)*

This was the former Catholic Apostolic Church, Victoria Street, that was used by the Elim Church from 1945 onwards. The building dated from about 1870. The Catholic Apostolic church was a strongly Adventist denomination that originated in America, but had waned in importance by the turn of the twentieth century and the reason for the survival of the church in West Bromwich is something of a mystery. *(Kevin Turner Collection)*

The Elim Church in Victoria Street, West Bromwich, now known as the West Bromwich Community Church, celebrated its seventieth birthday on 23 September 2006, and welcomed a new pastor Iain Hesketh (seen here at the door) with Pam Mason and Adrian Turner. *(NW)*

Pam Mason addresses members and friends at the West Bromwich Elim Church's seventieth anniversary. In the front row, in a white shirt, is Pastor John Glass who was pastor at West Bromwich from 1975 to 1980, but in 2006 was the General Superintendent of the Elim movement. He later addressed the meeting and took part in inducting the new pastor, Iain Hesketh. *(NW)*

In 1976 members of the Elim Church in West Bromwich campaigned in Wednesbury and established a fellowship that met for a time in Wednesbury Town Hall. Eventually this building in Crankhall Lane, Friar Park, was purchased. For a time the Wednesbury Elim Church operated independently but has now amalgamated with the West Bromwich Community Church to become one church again (but on two sites).

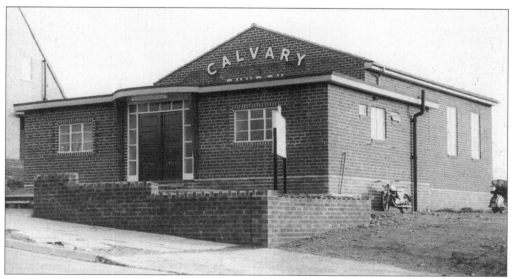

The Elim Church in Dudhill Road, Rowley Regis, was opened in 1959 as an independent fellowship. Mr and Mrs Bennett, who lived on the Brickhouse Farm Estate, felt called to plant this church here while attending a Pentecostal church in Cradley. Albert Bennett was joined by Hubert Haywood and Percy Smith in financing and building the church, to which they gave the name Calvary.

*Left:* Mrs Polly Pritchard, Mayor of Rowley Regis, came along on Saturday 10 October 1959 to open Calvary in Dudhill Road, escorted by her chauffeur. On the left are Albert Bennett, Hubert Hayward and on the right is Percy Smith with the microphone. The opening service was conducted by Pastor Gordon Cove, seen elsewhere in this book in the section on the Seagers Lane church in Brierley Hill.

In the mid-1960s a pastor was appointed who took the church into the Assemblies of God but by the early 1970s the congregation had dwindled and the church in Dudhill Road was struggling. The trustees decided to ask the Elim Church organisation to come to their assistance. Since Easter 1974 it has been an Elim Church, and says so on the front of the building where the words Calvary Church were once found. A few people joined the fellowship having come from Dudley's Elim Church in North Street.

The first Sunday School at Calvary. Behind the children are Albert Bennett, Percy Smith and the Revd Tony Stone. Albert's wife is sitting just in front of the Revd Stone. Albert Bennett, founder of the church, is still alive at the time of writing and still lives on the Brickhouse Farm Estate. The photographs of this church come from his collection.

# 11 Bethels & the Assemblies of God

The Welsh Revival, for example the work of evangelists like Evan Roberts, established a Pentecostal form of Christian witness at the beginning of the twentieth century. As the name implies, this revival mainly took place in Wales. However many young converts at these crusades became important evangelists in their own right and took their crusades to many other parts of the British Isles. It seems particularly relevant to consider the work of the Jeffreys: the brothers George Jeffreys (1889–1962) and Stephen Jeffreys (1876–1943) and the latter's son Edward (1899–1974).

As we noted in the previous chapter, George Jeffreys created the Elim Pentecost Church and held successful campaigns at Birmingham's Bingley Hall. Stephen joined the Elim movement in 1922 but four years later he transferred his allegiance to the emerging Assemblies of God.

The Assemblies of God had been created in 1924 at a gathering in Birmingham and by 1930 George was working on their behalf on a world tour. It was therefore his son, Edward Jeffreys, who led the crusade to the Black Country in 1930. By that time Edward had created the Bethel Evangelistic Society. In the wake of his crusade some converts set up Assembly of God fellowships. Some became part of the Bethel Movement and some were independent. It became more complicated after the collapse of the BES and some Bethels became Assemblies of God. Later still some Assembly of God fellowships became independent of the Assemblies of God.

Edward Jeffreys leading his 1930 crusade. It began in Walsall Town Hall from 24 February to 10 March, then moved on for a fortnight in Wednesbury Town Hall. From 24 March to 7 April it was in Dudley Town Hall and then moved to West Bromwich for a fortnight. While in each of these town halls the crusade also made quick visits to other local towns. The packed meetings drew people from all denominations and non-believers. Many local churches were hostile to the whole thing – particularly suspicious of the faith healing element and the talking in tongues. Others welcomed the Christian awakening that took place and the resulting conversions.

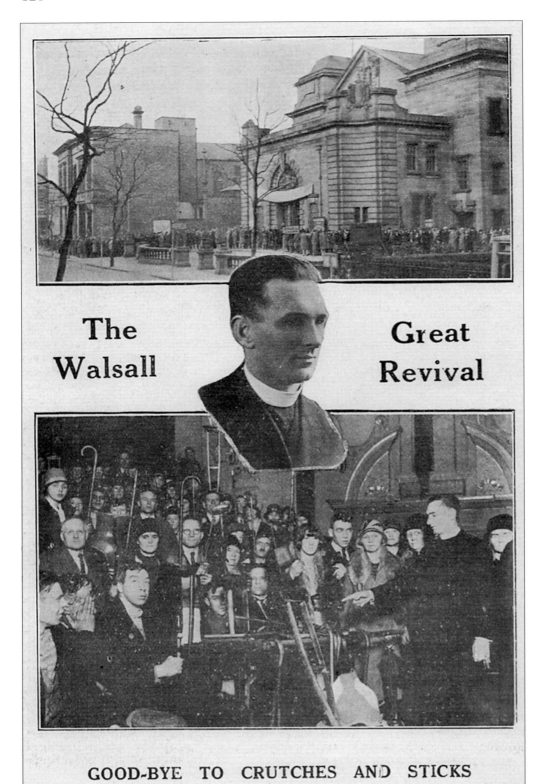

The Walsall    Great Revival

GOOD-BYE TO CRUTCHES AND STICKS

One problem faced by the Jeffreys crusade was what to do with the converts. Some returned to the churches to which they had formerly belonged, but sometimes found that they no longer fitted in. Others formed the potential membership of a Pentecostal fellowship. Edward Jeffreys appointed pastors who would stay behind as the crusade moved on and who assisted converts in finding a new spiritual home. In Walsall an assembly grew up which did not join the Bethel movement, in West Bromwich the opposite happened. In Dudley one group moved towards forming a Bethel Temple, while another became an Assembly of God.

As the Jeffreys crusade finished in West Bromwich on 21 April 1930 Pastor Rees Griffiths formed a fellowship which met until Whitsun in a local Congregational chapel. After Whitsun they moved to a field in Bromford Lane and awaited the arrival of a tent which can be seen in the above photograph. While using the tent, plans were made to provide a permanent building. Mr F. Carter advised on erecting an iron or steel frame to be clad in corrugated iron, with a Belfast roof and wooden panels on the interior walls. This was built quite quickly and the fellowship moved into their Bethel Temple in Gads Lane at the end of October 1930.

Pastor Rees Griffiths moved to West Bromwich in 1930 to continue the work of the Jeffreys Crusade. In calling the building in Gads Lane the Bethel Temple, he made it clear that further churches would be planted under the wing of Gads Lane. He pioneered the work that established a fellowship at Marsh Lane, West Bromwich, and conducted a mission in Great Bridge. The latter produced a Sunday School but did not grow to become a Bethel. There were also missions in Coseley and in Pensnett. In 1935, following the collapse of Edward Jeffrey's Bethel Evangelistic Society, the Gads Lane Assembly joined the Assemblies of God, pastored by Rees Griffiths until his death in 1949.

The members of the Bethel Temple, Gads Lane, built a platform outside their new temple to pose for this photograph, and assembled again inside for the photograph below. The construction of the building is shown quite well. The above picture shows the cladded sidewalls that could later be bricked and the brick frontage on the left. The picture below shows the Belfast roof to good advantage. The white dresses of the crusaders can be seen, and their practice of wearing hats. *(Pastor Graham Field)*

In 1967 the modernising of the Bethel Temple, Gads Lane, began and the side walls were bricked up. In its new guise it was reopened on 25 May 1968. In February 1972 the pastorate of David Skelton began and the temple began another period of expansion. At the beginning of 1979 construction of an extension seen on the left of the photograph below was commenced. On 24 May 1980 this extension was opened by the church treasurer, Mr F. Boden. He is seen in the top photograph opening the doors to the extension. Pastor David Skelton stands next to him. The front of the building has now been altered again by the addition of a modern porch. *(Pastor Graham Field)*

Pastor Rees Griffiths was a busy man in the wake of the 1930 Jeffreys crusade. While establishing himself in West Bromwich, and becoming pastor to the Gads Lane assembly, he also worked in Wednesbury, where he was assisted by Pastor Element, and in Dudley where he was assisted by Pastor Thrush, and we have already mentioned missions to Great Bridge, Coseley and Pensnett. Once established at Gads Lane, the mission to Marsh Lane began. As this is the only one to survive until the present day, it deserves to be dealt with next.

The Jeffreys crusade produced many converts throughout the West Bromwich area. The folks at Gads Lane were keen to help their colleagues in the Friar Park and Stone Cross areas to establish a mission out in the sticks. Here we see Mrs Griffiths, watched by Pastor Rees Griffiths, cutting the first turf in an empty field which was to be the location of a wooden building to be known, at first, as the Crankhall Mission in May 1932. Christmas services were held there in 1932 although the building was not completed until 1933.

No picture of the original wooden Crankhill Mission has been found, but after the Second World War, under the pastorship of Lesley Robinson, the building was bricked and reroofed. In this form it can be seen behind the Sunday School parade of the early 1950s at the foot of the opposite page. During the 1950s the Sunday School continued to grow and could not be contained in the building. Anniversaries had to be held in Charlemont Road School, as seen in this mid-1950s photograph.

By the mid-1950s the former Crankhill Mission was known as Marsh Lane. Here we see a Sunday School anniversary parade of the time led by the Royal Rovers band, led by David Paulton and Sidney Nicholls, a church elder.

The 1955 Marsh Lane Sunday School anniversary parade lines up in Marsh Lane itself. Alan Perry on the left (with the bugle) was son of Harry Perry, the Sunday School superintendent. (*David Paulton*)

Having become independent from Gads Lane in 1968, the Marsh Lane Pentecostal Church (Assemblies of God) built a new hall capable of holding 150 people, built by G.H. Phillips of West Bromwich. Here we see people gathering for the opening in June 1973. (*David Paulton*)

Mrs Isherwood, senior member of the congregation, turns the key to open the new Marsh Lane building in June 1973. She is surrounded by pastors and elders whose names soon become familiar to anyone studying the history of local Pentecostal churches. Left to right: Clifford Beasley (Oldbury), Fred Newcome (chief of the district), Gerald Chamberlain (Eve Lane), Harry Perry (Sunday School superintendent), Hector Evans (former pastor at Gads Lane), Mrs Isherwood, Caleb Beardsmore (Eve Lane), David Paulton with accordion, David Skelton (Gads Lane), Percy Griffiths (Bearwood) and Charles Element. The new building provided a vestibuled entrance, a heightened and enlarged space for worship, plus vestry, kitchen and toilets. *(David Paulton)*

The Marsh Lane Gospel Choir in their new 1973 building about two years after the opening. *(David Paulton)*

Ten years after the 1973 rebuild, the Marsh Lane Pentecostal Church doubled in size again. This new building, built by Robert Shaw of Wolverhampton, provides accommodation for 300, and was erected at a cost of £130,000. Since then it has undergone further slight modification but here we see it awaiting the opening in September 1983.

The 1983 opening was undertaken by Mrs Paulton, Mrs Hayes and Mrs Isherwood who stands on the right next to David Paulton. Once again Mrs Isherwood is surrounded by Assembly of God pastors. Compare with the 1973 opening on the previous page.

The congregation at the Marsh Lane Pentecostal Church seen outside their new building in September 1983, and below seated in the new building – the interior of which is seen to good effect in this picture of David Paulton addressing the assembly. The provision of a gallery plays a part in being able to accommodate 300 people. *(David Paulton)*

In the same way that Pastor Rees Griffiths came to West Bromwich to deal with the aftermath of the 1930 Jeffreys crusade, Pastor Richard Lewis came to Oldbury. He was another convert from the days of the Welsh Revival, but as part of Edward Jeffreys' team was part of the Bethel movement rather than part of the Assemblies of God. Once in Oldbury, Pastor Lewis lodged with Sam Element, a partner in the well-known firm of T. and S. Element, canal carriers. Sam was crippled with arthritis. He went to one of the crusade meetings – 'went with his sticks and came out without them'. As a result of the friendship

established between Sam Element and Pastor Lewis, they set out to provide Oldbury with a Bethel Pentecostal Temple. It was a wooden building, erected in New Street, and in the above picture Pastor Lewis and his wife pose outside the Bethel with the crusaders soon after the opening.

Ron and Anne Element of the Bethel Christian Fellowship in Oldbury, seen here in 2006. Anne's grandfather was Pastor Richard Lewis who came to Oldbury after the Jeffreys crusade of 1930, and Ron's grandfather was Sam Element, who provided Richard Lewis with lodgings and then was converted and helped him build the chapel. (NW)

A Sunday School anniversary at the Bethel Temple in New Street, Oldbury. Pastor Lewis and his wife are standing in the pulpit. The hall had been opened on the last Saturday of 1930. Mrs Element turned the key while Pastor Lewis led the singing of a hymn. During the evening Edward Jeffreys himself preached in the new building.

Pastor Lewis was at the Bethel Temple, Oldbury, until 1950 and died a year later on 2 February 1951. In this picture taken in January 1957 we see his son Edgar Lewis (on the left) taking part in unveiling a commemorative plaque in memory of his parents. With him are Pastor J.H. Hunt and Mr Hopla.

The wooden Bethel Temple in Oldbury lasted until 1970 and then had to be demolished to make way for a new Magistrates' Court. Left: On 23 April 1970 we see the treasurer, Fred Element, laying the foundation stone of a £26,000 replacement to be built on an adjacent site in Stone Street. On 21 November 1970 the congregation was able to walk from the old chapel to the new one. The building has been extended twice since then.

When Edward Jeffreys left the Bethel Evangelistic Society about 1932–3, the assembly in Oldbury remained affiliated to the Bethel Evangelistic Society, rather than turn to the Elim Church or the Assemblies of God. Today it still retains the word Bethel in its present name – the Bethel Christian Fellowship. One of its present claims to fame is that the pastor, Ken Hipkiss, is also chaplain to West Bromwich Albion FC. The Stone Street building can be seen in this picture of the congregation taken early in 2007. (*Both Bethel Temple/Christian Fellowship photographs Ron and Anne Element*)

The Bethel Full Gospel Hall, as it was originally called, in Stokes Street, Bloxwich, had an unusual history in that it was built in the wake of Edward Jeffreys' crusade of 1930. It was eventually closed only to be rescued and reopened as a church affiliated to the Assemblies of God. It is seen here as it was when opened on 30 April 1932 in the care of Pastor Wright who had begun Bloxwich-based meetings in the local Drill Hall. He bought the land and had it built. Eventually his health declined, the congregation dwindled and the building closed in 1964. A couple of years later the building was discovered by Jennie and Elsie Wood from the Assembly of God Fellowship in Temple Street, Wolverhampton. The sisters decided it should refurbished and reopened. (See page 130 of *More Black Country Chapels*).

A pre-war pantomime presented by members of the Bloxwich Gospel Hall.

*Above:* Elsie Wood takes a break while rescuing the abandoned Bethel Gospel Hall in Bloxwich.
*Right:* Pastor Wright who had nurtured, built and cared for the hall from 1932 until the mid-1950s. He was an ex-Welsh miner – injured in the pit, who was healed and saved by Edward Jeffreys.

It took about seventeen weeks to restore the building in Stokes Road, Bloxwich, after it had been purchased by the Wood sisters. Work on the outside of the building (above) and inside was completed ready for an opening in August 1967. Under the pastorship of the Wood sisters it then became known as Bloxwich Pentecostal Church.

A late 1990s refurbishment, seen below, lowered the ceiling of the building and modernised it. *(Neville Johnson Collection)*

The church in Stokes Street, Bloxwich, later became known as the Bloxwich New Life Centre, and under the pastorship of Neville Johnson was refurbished in the late 1990s. In January 2005 it changed its name once again to become the Bloxwich Community Church, but during all this time it has remained affiliated to the Assemblies of God. *(NW)*

In March 1930 the *Dudley Herald* printed this picture of the queues building up at Dudley Town Hall as people waited to be admitted to a meeting of the Jeffreys crusade. On some nights the queue stretched to Castle Hill!

## The Jeffreys crusade and its aftermath in Dudley

The events of spring 1930 were recorded in a booklet by Pastor Matthew Francis, who led an independent evangelical church which had grew out of the Walsall crusade, until his death in 1954. The booklet is called ;The Omnipotence of Faith; and includes dramatic pictures of queues forming outside the town halls of Walsall, Wednesbury and Dudley during the crusades. As well as quotations from reports in the *Dudley Herald* and *Birmingham Mail*, the booklet includes independent observations from Idris Williams, a Baptist minister from Cradley Heath, and Bert Bissell from Dudley's Vicar Street Young Men's Class. (See pages 93 and 94 of *More Black Country Chapels*).

Idris Williams, who also produced a decent history of chapels in the Cradley Heath area, invited Edward Jeffreys to appear in Cradley Heath's Whitley Memorial Hall on Wednesday 26 March 1930. Bert Bissell did not invite Edward Jeffreys to Vicar Street, but was equally positive about the nature and success of the crusade. He acknowledged the extent to which it had raised local interest in Christianity, was proving beneficial to local churches and chapels, and was genuine in its demonstrations of faith healing. Many critics were dismissive of the faith healing aspects of these crusades but Bert, who spent several hours in the company of Edward Jeffreys, defended it and spoke warmly in praise of Jeffreys as an individual.

While compiling this book it has been possible to talk to Ron Shaw who is now ninety-six but was present at the Edward Jeffreys crusade in Dudley Town Hall. Ron's salvation and his desire to save others and share the 'Pentecostal Experience' is still very evident three-quarters of a century later. Here, we are able to follow four stories of events that followed the crusade. Firstly there was a Bethel Fellowship established in Dudley, secondly and thirdly there are Assemblies of God which still exist today (Salop Street and Eve Lane), and fourthly there is the story of Ann Brown's mission to Quarry Bank.

Pastor Rees Griffiths, while establishing himself at Gads Lane, West Bromwich, also worked in Dudley immediately after the Jeffreys crusade to help converts who wished to build a Bethel assembly in the town. Finding accommodation was not easy and they first met in a room in New Street. Later they moved to another 'Upper Room' at the rear of the yard reached from the arched entry in Salop Street seen in the above picture. This Bethel meeting was pastored by Pastor Thrush, then Pastor Davison and a Mr Hall. When it closed its few surviving members joined the other Pentecostal fellowship established in Salop Street. *(Lilian Sheldon)*

Two converts saved at the Jeffreys' town hall meetings of 1930 were Joseph Giles and Kate Mansell. Later they married but in the immediate aftermath of the crusade Joseph frequently travelled to Wales to undertake further Bible study. At some stage they felt the call to establish a Dudley Pentecostal Church – though why this had to be separate from the Bethel fellowship is not clear. Joseph Giles began his pastorate in an upper room in premises in Cross Street in about 1934. When the fellowship outgrew the premises they moved to Park Road, and then at the end of the war to a site in Salop Street. In the above picture Joseph and Kate lead a DIY construction gang at Salop Street.

By 1949 the Dudley Pentecostal Church in Salop Street was complete, having constructed a sectional building on a DIY basis. The congregation pose here with Pastor Giles on the extreme right, next to his father. Close to them is Mr Payton who provided some of the carpentry and joinery skills, and his son Brian. Brian reappears in a 2004 picture taken in Netherton on page 101 of *Black Country Chapels* – such is the small world of chapel history! *(Mavis Ainsbury)*

The Salop Street Pentecostal Church ran a successful Sunday School, members of which are seen here in the 1970s. *(Mavis Ainsbury)*

In the mid-1970s the Salop Street fellowship, during the pastorship of Gerald Chamberlain, moved to its present home on the opposite side of the road. The Dudley Christian Fellowship, as it is now called, was opened on 3 April 1976 by Kath Giles, the widow of Joseph Giles. The Mayor of Dudley, Cllr Jack Wilson, was also present as the £62,000 church was opened. The old British Oak public house has been acquired by the Fellowship as an annex and forms the foreground of this 2007 picture. *(NW)*

Another strand of the story of what happened after the Jeffreys Crusade left Dudley Town Hall in 1930 is the tale of Mrs Ann Brown, of Occupation Street, Dudley, seen on the right. Ann Brown had been a member of St James's Church, Eve Hill, but was saved at Dudley Town Hall, and then devoted her life to the salvation of others.

She became Sister Brown and began to look for a site where she might establish her own Pentecostal congregation. The rather damaged photograph was provided by Joe Chattin who later had to carry on Sister Brown's work. *(Joe Chattin)*

## The Bethany Temple, Mount Pleasant, Quarry Bank

Sister Brown's Bethany Temple was a small wooden building erected on ground between Talbot Lane and Mount Pleasant, close to coal pits that were being worked by Tinker Round. Mr Brown was chauffeur to the Earl of Dudley and it was this connection that apparently persuaded the Earl to sell Sister Brown the plot. The *Dudley Herald* of 11 August 1934 is the first to mention the Bethany Temple and it must have opened sometime during that summer.

The fellowship grew and Sister Ann Brown was hard working and an inspired leader. The congregation eventually included a Mr Pearson from West Street, Quarry Bank, who had useful building skills. He was able to introduce some ironwork that gave the building greater stability, and was able to enlarge the building. A small wooden tea-room was built along side the main wooden structure, and the surrounding ground became a garden. At some stage some impressive iron gates were erected at the Talbot Lane entrance. The Browns would spend their weekends on the site, having journeyed to the Bethany by bus.

Just before the Second World War a young man named Joe Chattin came to the Bethany Temple and later brought his friend Cyril Baker who eventually became a pastor at Amblecote and Brierley Hill. Joe Chattin came to live with the Browns after the war and helped in the work at the Bethany. Sister Brown's health declined in the early 1960s and after her death on 15 September 1964, Joe continued to run the Bethany for as long as he could, while working for the MEB. New factories grew up around it, and the land it occupied sometimes flooded. They were difficult times.

Although there had been a reasonable congregation in the 1950s it declined after Sister Brown's death and in 1974 someone set fire to the building. There seemed no prospect of rebuilding the Bethany Temple and Joe Chattin had to relinquish it. The land was sold and a developer relandscaped and drained it and factories have grown up on the site. Sister Brown's choice of name may have been significant. It appears to have been a totally independent venture without affiliation to the Bethel Evangelistic Society or to the Assemblies of God.

Pictures of the Bethany Temple in Talbot Lane, Quarry Bank, do not seem to have survived. The side of the temple can just be glimpsed in this post-war picture of Sunday School at the Bethany. *(Joe Chattin)*

## The Eve Lane Pentecostal Church, Upper Gornal

Another convert at the Jeffreys crusade in Dudley Town Hall was Caleb Beardsmore, a cobbler from Upper Gornal. He joined the Bethel fellowship that Pastor Rees Griffiths was trying to establish in Dudley in 1930. Along with Pastor Thrush, he moved from New Street to the room in Salop Street, but soon felt the call to establish a fellowship in Upper Gornal. Meetings began at his house in Kent Street, and then, in 1936, it became possible to move into an upper room above an old bakehouse in Eve Lane.

In 1939 a church was built on the site of the old bakehouse, which opened just before the Second World War broke out. This building is seen in the above picture and was built by Pastor Toon who combined building work with being a pastor. Caleb continued to lead the fellowship until the early 1960s and remained an advisor until his death in 1982, aged ninety-three.

In the 1970s there was much talk about replacing the 1939 building and this was finally accomplished in 1984, built by Shaw Ltd of Coseley. The fellowship at Eve Lane has played a part in helping establish other churches at Sedgley, Kingswinford, Wombourne and at 'Junction 10'.

The 1984 Eve Lane Pentecostal Church as it looks today. (NW)

## The aftermath of the Jeffreys crusade in Walsall

It has already been mentioned that Pastor Matthew Francis was one of the evangelists working with Edward Jeffreys as the latter swept through the Black Country in 1930. Matthew Francis chronicled the crusade in his booklet, 'The Omnipotence of Faith', and was the man who Edward Jeffreys asked to stay behind as the crusade moved on from Walsall to other parts of the Black Country.

Matthew Francis, born in Llanelli in 1886, was a powerful preacher, with a background in the Welsh Revival, some Salvation Army training and close association with the Bethel Evangelistic Society and Edward Jeffreys. He continued to hold meetings in Walsall Town Hall. When the town hall was not available, the congregation moved to the De Luxe Cinema in Stafford Street, or His Majesty's Theatre at Town End Bank. There were also open-air services, and formation of Crusaders and Sunbeams.

The Wesleyan Chapel in Queen Street had become redundant to a declining congregation and was readily sold to the Bethel movement. Mrs Francis reopened the building as the Bethel Temple on Monday 21 March 1930, and ten days later Edward Jeffreys himself came to preach there. Matthew Francis was its first pastor, a role which had to be carried out alongside an increasing number of other responsibilities within the Bethel movement.

When the Bethel Evangelistic Society collapsed in 1932 Matthew Francis took the Queen Street congregation out of the movement. He led his Queen Street chapel, simply known as 'The Temple', as an independent congregation until his death on 22 May 1954.

Five years elapsed before the Temple found a successor to Pastor Mathews. Keith Tanner, who arrived in 1959 faced a number of difficulties including the future of the Queen Street building. This was resolved in a complicated series of events. The outcome was that the (Queen Street) Temple took over a Brethren Hall built on the Beechdale Estate. The hall, known as 'Stephenson Hall' had been opened in 1958, but became home to the Queen Street folk in March 1964 (see page 62).

Six years after the move to Beechdale, Keith Tanner died. He was followed by Pastor Neville Swain. Listing the names of pastors and ministers has not been a feature of these books, but in this case the history of the Walsall Independent Evangelical Church (three locations and four pastors) there seems to be a special link between the congregation's history and the influence of their pastor. Between the third pastorate of Neville Swain and the fourth pastorate of Will Loescher, there was a period of joint leadership by these two men at Beechdale. During this period the question of leaving the estate and becoming a town centre congregation once again began to gain momentum. In September 1997 services at the Walsall Independent Evangelical Church began in the former Territorial Army building in Bath Street. The connection with Beechdale gradually faded and the work first established by Matthew Francis is now firmly consolidated at the Bath Street Centre.

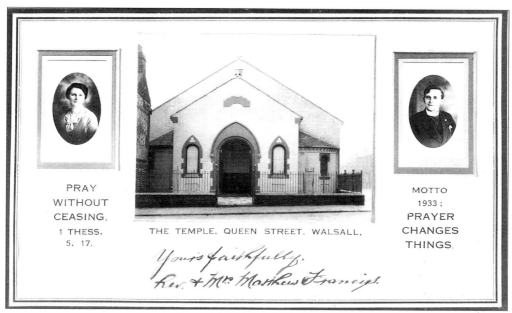

PRAY
WITHOUT
CEASING.
1 THESS.
5. 17.

THE TEMPLE. QUEEN STREET. WALSALL.

MOTTO
1933 :
PRAYER
CHANGES
THINGS.

The Revd Matthew Francis has signed the front of this card featuring a picture of himself and his wife plus a rare view of the Regent Street building. It was first a Wesleyan Methodist Chapel then a Bethel Temple, opened in the wake of the Jeffreys crusades visit to Walsall in the 1930s. From 1932 on wards it was simply 'The Temple' and survived as such until 1964 when the congregation moved to the Stephenson Hall on the Beechdale Estate. *(WIEC)*

The Pentecostal fellowship established by Francis Matthews in the Regent Street Temple is now represented by the congregation meeting in the Bath Street building seen above in this 2006 picture. After a sojourn on the Beechdale Estate, the Walsall Independent Evangelical Church, as it has now become known, moved into this ex-Territorial Army building in 1977. The first service was held on Saturday 6 September 1997, the day of Princess Diana's funeral. *(WIEC)*

## A complicated story from Amblecote

It seems a big leap from Walsall in the east of the Black Country to Amblecote in the west, but in each we find a Pentecostal church established in the aftermath of the Jeffreys crusade which goes through the same progress to eventual independence of both the Bethel Movement and the Assemblies of God.

A fellowship first started in Stourbridge after the 1930 Jeffreys crusade was able to move to Amblecote when premises became available in Dial Lane. In about 1940 they moved once again and went to the old Mission Hall in King William Street, Amblecote. This building had been opened as the Dennis Park Mission by Trinity – the Anglican parish church in Amblecote – on 15 January 1889. A foundation stone had been laid on 27 September 1888 and this has now returned to Trinity to form part of the end wall of the Church Hall of 1922! As far as the Assembly of God fellowship was concerned, the building was rented from Mr Squires of Stourbridge who had bought it from the Church of England. By the end of the 1950s it seemed to be in decline and the pastor, the Revd Billy Buckley, was considering its closure. Mr Squires had expressed an interest in converting the building into a warehouse. The council rejected that possibility, Mr Squires died, and the building ended up being for sale.

Once again we find that a new pastor helps bring about a change of direction. Cyril Baker became pastor in 1960 and one of his first tasks was to actually purchase the King William Street building and begin its renovation. The hall acquired a new ceiling and Cyril acquired some second-hand cinema seats for 5s each, and the old mission was given a new lease of life.

In 1967 Cyril Baker moved to a new challenge at Seagers Lane but the assembly at King William Street prospered and in 1979 moved to larger premises – the old Methodist Church in Brettell Lane.

The King William Street Mission, Amblecote, as it appeared in 2006. It has slipped into anonymity as a number plate factory, and is hidden by surrounding buildings. (NW)

Photographs of the life and times of the King William Street Mission seem to be rare. This rather creased snap reveals the front of the building's interior. The scroll carries the legend: 'Jesus Christ the same yesterday and today and forever'. Certainly the King William Street building seems to go on forever. It survives today as a number plate factory. Also note the cinema seats that Cyril Baker managed to purchase when modernising the hall in 1960. *(Bill Webb Collection)*

A happy scene at the King William Street Mission in July 1977 after the dedication of Phil Cook's son, seen here in his mother's arms. Not long after this the congregation had to start using the Adult Training Centre in Brettell Lane for Sunday worship as the decision had been made to buy the old Methodist Church in Brettell Lane and much work had to be done on it before moving in. *(Phil Cook)*

In 1979 the Assembly of God fellowship in King William Street, Amblecote, bought these two buildings in Brettell Lane. The building on the right was known as 'the coach-house' but the chapel on the left had an interesting history. The first chapel built on this site – back in 1831 – belonged to the Wesleyan Methodists. In 1836, as a result of a split, the chapel became Methodist New Connexion and the Wesleyans were forced to start again around the corner in High Street. The Methodists here in Brettell Lane struggled on until August 1957 and then went to join the folks in High Street. At some stage the building was then leased to Christian Scientists. Once acquired by the Assembly of God fellowship, much refurbishment had to take place and it was finally reopened in the guise seen here on 5 September 1981 as the Amblecote Full Gospel Church.

The interior of the Amblecote Full Gospel Church, Brettell Lane, after its refurbishment by the Assembly of God fellowship, completed in 1981. (*Bill Webb/Phil Cook Collection*)

The Amblecote Christian Centre, Brettell Lane, 2007.

History repeated itself and the Assembly of God fellowship outgrew the ex-Methodist Church on this site. For eighteen months at the beginning of the 1990s, services were held at King Edward College in Stourbridge while the old building was demolished and this replacement was built.

It opened as the Amblecote Christian Centre on 14 February 1993. Since then it has ceased to be affiliated to the Assemblies of God and has become independent, although it does belong to an inter-denominational network called 'The Net'.

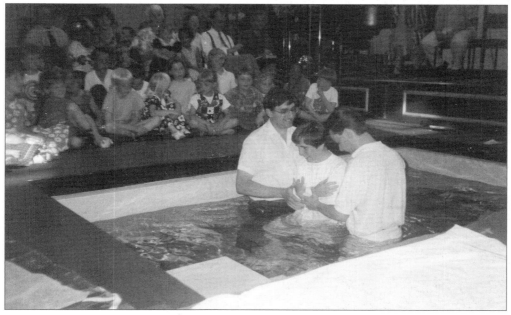

Pastor Phil Cook performs a baptism at the Amblecote Christian Centre in the 1990s. It is interesting to compare this photograph with another of a baptism performed by Pastor Cove at Seagers Lane on page 11 of *Black Country Chapels*. Baptism by total immersion is a essential feature of Gospel Hall and Pentecostal church life. *(Phil Cook Collection)*

## The Assemblies of God in Brierley Hill

In 1950 Pastor Cove, an Assemblies of God minister, brought the 'Midnight Hour Campaign' to Stourbridge in the form of a tented crusade. Converts formed a house group which met in Wollaston and then Pastor Cove acquired the disued Mission Hall in Seagers Lane, Brierley Hill. The hall had to be cleaned up and refurbished and here we see it opening as the Glad Tidings Hall on Saturday 19 May 1951. Below: Pastor Sturgess of Tipton Assembly of God puts the key into the door of the Glad Tidings Hall, Seagers Lane, 19 May 1951. On the left, with the Bible under his arm, is Pastor Caleb Beardsmore from Eve Lane. On the right is Pastor Cove, with his hands behind his back. *(Bill Webb Collection)*

Pastor Gordon Cove and some members of the assembly inside the Glad Tidings Hall, Seagers Lane, Brierley Hill, 1950s.

The hall first opened on 24 March 1921 (see page 128 of *Black Country Chapels*). It was then called the People's Mission Hall and was established by David Poole who came from the Baptist Chapel in New Street, Dudley. In 1926 he started a Sunday School mission in an upper room in Brierley Hill High Street, followed by open-air meetings in Marsh Park. Success led to the building of the hall in nearby Seagers Lane. It was designed by local architect Stanley Griffiths and was formally opened by Cllr Chattin, chairman of the Urban District Council and JP.

As the People's Mission Hall, it declined and closed in the mid-1930s but from 1937 to 1946 it was used by a local Salvation Army Corps. Four years of disuse ended when Pastor Cove came on the scene. The Assembly of God fellowship subsequently expanded the building but closed it when it became possible to move to the ex-Congregational church in Albion Street in 1976. *(Bill Webb Collection)*

The hall at Seagers Lane could only be enlarged by adding side extensions to the original building. One extension was added in 1954, the other followed two years later. Other improvements followed as the congregation grew in size. *(Cyril Baker Collection)*

A baptismal service at Seagers Lane during Gordon Cove's pastorate. Left to right: Mrs Cove (at the piano), Jessie Thatcher, Mrs Wright, Joan Hingley, Mrs Colwell Snr and Mrs Brown await baptism. On their left is Mr Colwell Snr, who became a deacon of the church. On the right is Mr Foxall, who became church treasurer. *(Cyril Baker Collection)*

Pastor Cyril Baker appears fourth from left on the back row in this picture taken at Seagers Lane during his pastorate (1967–77). His wife, Mona, appears far left on the front row. The picture includes Les and Frank Colwell, wives, sons and daughters-in-law, etc. Assemblies of God fellowships, like those of the Gospel Halls, are very much family-connected. *(Cyril Baker Collection)*

In 1976 the Assembly of God fellowship at Seagers Lane, Brierley Hill, purchased the one-time Congregational church in Albion Street, and Cyril's son David Baker, became the pastor. The building, which dates from 1882, was in poor condition and much work was put in to make it serviceable. This photograph shows the building in pre-war condition, although the picture was still being used on the front of a 1963 church bazaar programme. The Assembly of God fellowship opened in Albion Street on 30 April 1977.

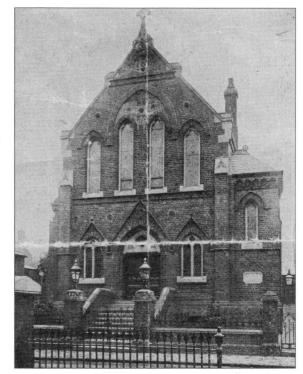

*Below:* A 1970s picture of Sunday School scholars at Albion Street. *(Both David Baker Collection)*

The interior of the Pentecostal Church, Albion Street, Brierley Hill, as it looks today. It was renovated by the Assemblies Of God fellowship from Seagers Lane. The ceiling has been lowered and the pulpit, spiral staircase and organ have been removed. For the time being the old Congregational chapel's pews remain in use, but they have been re-upholstered.

Pastor Cyril Baker who was youth leader at Eve Lane, went to King William Street in 1960 as pastor and was at Seagers Lane from 1967 to 1977. On the right is his son, David Baker, who is pastor at Albion Street. The pulpit comes from Bent Street Methodist Chapel. *(NW)*

# 12 Independent Evangelical Churches

All over the Black Country there are independent chapels and churches that are not part of a nationally- or even regionally-organised denomination. Some of them have been described in the previous two volumes but it seems impossible to feel that they have ever been comprehensively covered. A few more can be covered in this chapter. Meanwhile, I am always discovering new ones.

Some of the independent fellowships and congregations have become independent after leaving a more established grouping – such as the Amblecote Christian Centre which has left the Assemblies of God. Others were independent from the start but were established by a group of people leaving a congregation that had been part of a recognised denomination, such as he People's Mission Halls at Swan Street, Netherton, and Seagers Lane, Brierley Hill, and the Hall Street Gospel Hall in Willenhall. All three were started by people who had been Baptists. In the Willenhall example they then became associated with the Brethren. Over in Walsall the present congregation at the Bath Street Centre started out as part of the Bethel movement, later took over Brethren premises in Beechdale and has now returned to central Walsall as an independent. As such it is now part of the Federation of Independent Evangelical Churches *(FIEC)*.

If we list some of the existing local members of the FIEC, it will give some idea of the variety of congregations operating under this umbrella: Cradley Baptists at Church Road, Cradley; the Endowed School Mission, Rowley Regis (see page 38 of *More Black Country Chapels*); the Oakham Evangelical Church, City Road; Providence Church, Smethwick, the Straights Church, Gornal Wood; and the Wall Heath Evangelical Church, which has recently created an offshoot meeting at Crestwood.

The independent Evangelical church at Fatherless Barn, Cradley, was established 1957 by Arthur and Thelma Adams who came from Hanover Hall, Hanover Road (now Regis Christian Centre). Fatherless Barn Church is celebrating its fiftieth anniversary as this book goes to print. *(NW)*

# ACKNOWLEDGEMENTS

This book, and its two predecessors, could not have been written without the help of many people who have been generous with their time and resources. I would particularly like to thank the following:

Mavis Ainsbury, Olive Allchurch, Bernard Appleby, Carolyn Arnold, Cyril Baker, David Baker, Sheila Balgobin, Mrs D. Botterill, Ken and Hilda Buckler, Ray Bush, Les Burrows, Joe Chattin, Les and Winnie Churm, Phil Cook, Norman Cooksey, Barry Dale, Frank, Nancy and John Daniel, Doreen Davies, Lloyd and Margaret Davies, Eunice Eaves, Ron and Anne Element, John Evans, John Farrington, Derek Fellows, Graham Field, Iris Gamble, Peggy Groves, Betty Guy, Margaret Haden, Leslie Hardwick, Florence Harper, Gordon Hawkes, Dorothy Hicklin, Peter Hickman, Betty Hopkins, Elsie Horan, Joan Howes, Brian Hudson, Les Hunter, John James, Neville and June Johnson, Fred Jones, Jo Kelford, the Revd Tony Kinch, Ron Lake, Betty Lavender, Will Loesher, Barbara Lowe, Eric Maley, Kevin Manning, Leigh Maydew, Marion Palmer, Bev Parker, David and Doreen Paulton, Brian Payton, the Revd Alan Penduck, Keith Perry, Anne and David Pitt, David Phillips, Alan Price, Frank Preece, the Revd Paul Rock, Tony Sankey, Moira Simpson, Ron Shaw, John and Sheila Smart, Bill Smith, Freda Smith, Gillian Snaith, Margaret Stanley, Margaret Taylor, Ann Thomas, Derek Trickett, Kevin and Denise Turner, Neil Walker, Ray Walker, Bill Webb, Margaret Weston, David and Dawn Woodman, Roger Wootton, John Wilmore, Judith Wilson, Joy Winkworth and Graham Wycherley.

So many people have assisted me, I fear that there must be names I have missed. As usual, special mention must be made of Terri Baker Mills who has provided moral support throughout all stages of the production of this book.

And the chapels that got away? Three chapters of this book had be omitted because they would not fit. Sections on Tividale, Pensnett, and the Lye, plus material on the Independent Evangelicals remain 'in abeyance'. The Methodist Chapel in Dudley Street West, Tividale, dated from 1840, but was derelict at the time this photograph was taken in 1977. The last service had taken place on 19 December 1976. Thirty years later it serves to remind us that the subject of local chapel history is vast and defies the attempt to fit it into three volumes! (*Ann Thomas*)